BRITTNEI FARMER

God is Keeping Me
Copyright © 2025 by Brittnei Farmer

All rights reserved. This book or any portion thereof may not be reproduced or used in any manner whatsoever without the express written permission of the publisher except for the use of brief quotations in a book review.

Limits of Liability and Disclaimer of Warranty
The author and publisher shall not be liable for your misuse of this material. This book is strictly for informational purposes. The purpose of this book is to educate. The author and publisher do not guarantee anyone following these techniques, suggestions, tips, ideas, or strategies will become successful. The author and publisher shall have neither liability nor responsibility to anyone with respect to any loss or damage caused, or alleged to be caused, directly or indirectly by the information contained in this book. Views expressed in this publication do not necessarily reflect the views of the publisher.

This is a work of creative nonfiction. The events are portrayed to the best of Brittnei Farmer's memory. While all the stories in this book are true, some names and identifying details have been changed to protect the privacy of the people involved.

Photographer: Brandon Farmer

Printed in the United States of America
Keen Vision Publishing, LLC
www.publishwithkvp.com
ISBN: 979-8-9927392-9-9

For my loving and supportive parents,
Ed and Jackie Farmer.

CONTENTS

God is Keeping Me (Poetic Praise)	7
Introduction	10
Chapter One	14
Chapter Two	18
Chapter Three	22
Chapter Four	25
Chapter Five	30
Chapter Six	36
Chapter Seven	43
Chapter Eight	46
Chapter Nine	53
Chapter Ten	56
Chapter Eleven	59
Chapter Twelve	65
Chapter Thirteen	71
Chapter Fourteen	75
Chapter Fifteen	77
You're Not Alone (Poem)	84
Chapter Sixteen	87
Chapter Seventeen	90
Chapter Eighteen	94
Chapter Nineteen	99
Chapter Twenty	102
Chapter Twenty-One	107
Chapter Twenty-Two	110

Chapter Twenty-Three	115
Chapter Twenty-Four	121
Chapter Twenty-Five	128
My Testimony	130
The Chosen One	138
About the Author	141
Connect with the Author	144

God is Keeping Me

As I look back over my life
And see what all I've been through.
I realized I never would have made it,
if it had not been for You.

The One who sent His only Son
to give His life just for me.
Who then rose three days later
so that I may be free.

My life has not been easy.
There were many bumps and bruises along the way.
Even the devil had crept in
And made it so hard to pray.

So-called friends let me down.
Some threw dirt on my name
Even fake friends stayed around
just to see what all they could gain.

I've had many health problems,
physical and mental, just to name a few.
And even being a woman of GOD,
yes, my spiritual health failed, too.

GOD IS KEEPING ME

I've lost many loved ones.
Grief sometimes too hard to bear.
I've even lost one in the worst way.
And I still don't think it was fair.

I've learned life throws you curved balls.
And a few fastballs, too.
But then the balls of life slow down,
just to show you what all GOD can do.

There were times in my life
when I couldn't see my way through.
And those were the times I knew
it was nobody but You.

Who kept me when I was down?
Who kept me when I did wrong?
Who kept me when I didn't even ask?
And that's the reason for my song.

GOD is keeping me
through my trials and through my tests.
And GOD is still keeping me,
even through all of my mess.

GOD has been so good to me.
He answers every time I call.
He's better to me than I am to myself.
Lord, I just can't tell it all.

There's an anointing on my life.
I don't know why GOD has chosen me.
To be the recipient of so many blessings,
way beyond what my eyes can see.

So, I'll go forth and spread Your Word
And teach how Holy is Your Name.
I'll remind Your people of King Jesus
for us sinners is the reason why He came.

Because of Your mercy and amazing grace
this race, I'll continue to run.
Until I see my Savior face to face,
and hear You say, "Well Done!"

Introduction

Every day we wake up is a blessing from GOD. Tomorrow is never promised to us. So much can happen at a moment's notice. If your house is not in order, may GOD save your soul.

1, 2, 3, 4... Breathe.
1, 2, 3, 4, 5... Breathe.
1, 2, 3, 4,5, 6... Breathe.
1, 2, 3, 4, 5, 6, 7... Breathe.
1, 2, 3, 4, 5, 6, 7, 8... He's not breathing!
OH MY GOD, HE STOPPED BREATHING!!!

As I grabbed at his shoulders with his head in my lap, my life as I knew it would never be the same. At that very moment, as I witnessed my boyfriend transition to the other side, a piece of me died with him. I HURT!

An indescribable pain shot through my body and punctured my soul. I HURT! I had never felt a pain like this before. No pain would ever be able to compare.

INTRODUCTION

I HURT! My agony reached depths that I could not describe. I, Brittnei Michelle Farmer, was hurting, and there was nothing anyone could do about it.

It took the paramedics what seemed like forever for them to get there. They said they could not find the apartment number, so I had to leave Craig's side to meet them downstairs. I did not quite understand why it seemed as if everyone and everything was moving in slow motion. Even as I tried dialing his mother's number, my fingers were just stuck. They tried working on him in my living room for about 20 minutes.

Every time they shocked him with the defibrillator, I kept asking, "Is he breathing?"

I never got a response.

When they finally decided to take him out of the apartment, the urgency was gone. They were not rushing, nor was there much conversation between the paramedics. I knew he was gone. But yet and still, I held out a little hope that a miracle would happen or that I could finally wake up from this horrible nightmare. But when I attempted to get in the back of the ambulance with him, the little bit of my heart that held out any hope that they could save him burned out when they denied me access. He was gone. My future husband had passed away.

The trip to the hospital was a blur. After following behind the ambulance and running every red light with them, I finally pulled up to the hospital and got out. That's when I noticed my parking was that of someone learning how to drive. When I saw them rolling Craig in with everything covered but one arm hanging down from under the white sheet, I just looked up to the sky. I wanted to be angry with GOD. Not because He took Craig but because He left me.

However, GOD did not truly leave me — despite my feelings at the time. GOD will never put more on us than we can bear. Even though this might sound like a cliché, it is also true. GOD knows how much we can handle. Have you ever wondered how you managed to get through and overcome something while the entire time you kept thinking to yourself, there is no way I am going to get through this? NOBODY BUT GOD! Even in the midst of whatever it is we are dealing with, we are never going through it alone. Even when we find ourselves going in the opposite direction of what GOD has planned, He simply reroutes us and gets us back on the right track. No matter how many times we may turn our back on GOD, His arms are open and stretched out still. Now, who would not want to serve a GOD like that?

As soon as I started on this Christian journey, Satan came at me in every shape, form, and fashion. I have to admit, there were times I would get a little discouraged, tired, and sometimes impatient, but 2 Thessalonians 3:13 (KJV) reminds me, "*But ye, brethren, be not weary in well doing.*" I have also learned that suffering is a part of the package. So, with all of this being said, stay strong and be of good courage; you are not alone. Whether you

INTRODUCTION

have been on this journey for quite some time or just getting started, remember GOD will never leave you nor forsake you. Through it all, tell yourself, *GOD IS KEEPING ME!*

Chapter One

And if it seem evil unto you to serve the LORD, choose you this day whom ye will serve; whether the gods which your fathers served that were on the other side of the flood, or the gods of the Amorites, in whose land ye dwell: but as for me and my house, we will serve the LORD.

JOSHUA 24:15 (KJV)

I was born August 17, 1987, to Edward and Jacquelynn Farmer. I was their second child and second daughter. My sister, Brandi, who was two years old, was already not fond of me. She did not like me very much. In fact, I don't think she liked me at all. Still, I wanted a relationship with her anyway. I made friends easily, stayed out of trouble, and was a happy child. Even if I had no one to play with, I could always count on myself to have fun.

When I was six years old, we moved to Gulfport, MS. One day, not too long after moving into our new neighborhood, I met this girl named April while riding my bike. She was the first of many friends I would make soon after. I made many friends, and they always wanted to come to my house because there was always something to do. I was allowed to go to my friend's house as long as I had my homework and chores done. I also had to be home before the streetlights came on, or the punishments

CHAPTER ONE

would soon follow. Growing up, life was simple. Going to school and church was a must in our household. At an early age, my parents taught me the importance of having a relationship with GOD. I got my lessons in school as well as in church. We are members of Shiloh Missionary Baptist Church in Saucier, MS. Growing up, going to church did not mean much to me then, but as I got older, I understood it better by and by, like the song says. Truth be told, I hated getting up early on Sunday to go to church. However, I always looked forward to the naps that helped pass the time. When we reached a certain age, we were no longer allowed to sleep during service. When we did fall asleep, my dad would pinch us. As our eyes swelled and filled with tears, we were not to make a sound, or we were guaranteed to get another pinch. At that time, my mom would rub my arm and make me feel better.

My mom and I are so much alike. From our personalities to introverted characteristics, we are mirror images of one another — even down to our health issues, but that is another story. My mom has always been my backbone and the voice of reason between my dad and me, even though she is very soft-spoken. She would step in to keep the peace between us. As I got older, we grew closer, and our relationship became stronger. She is my confidant, my go-to person, my prayer warrior, and most importantly, my best friend. Lord, I could not ask for a better mother. On the other hand, my dad was the exact opposite of my mother. He ruled his house with an iron fist and did not care if we were upset with him for our punishment. Even though my dad had his stern ways, he loved his family unconditionally. With me being his baby girl, I was also a daddy's girl. Yes, I was spoiled! My dad is a true man of GOD. I have always admired the way he conducts himself in whatever situation he is in. Though, I could have done without some of those punishments. "Spare the rod, spoil the child" was the Scripture I believe he lived by. I thanked GOD when we outgrew the whippings. My dad is my protector, my provider, my "picker-upper," and most of all, my prayer warrior when times get hard. Despite his strict ways growing up, I would not trade him for anything in the world.

Outside of my immediate family, we were big in numbers and very family-oriented. We all know the power of prayer and believe that after GOD, family comes next. In addition to being a tight-knit family, our entire family has a very athletic background. The Farmers dominated in sports, whether football, basketball, baseball, or softball. The first year my parents signed me up for tee-ball, I just wanted to play in the sand with other kids. Of course, my dad was not happy since he had already paid and thought I would be a year behind. Little did he or anyone else know the athletic talent I possessed. I eventually played the following year, and, to everyone's surprise, I was actually pretty good. I loved the game, but I never expected how big an impact it would have on me later in life. My younger brother was

CHAPTER ONE

born March 24, 1994, and our family was complete. My parents finally had their 3 B's: Brandi, Brittnei, and Brandon. Everyone would always get our names mixed up and complain to our parents about why they named us so close together. Still, to this day, my sister and I get mistaken for one another. After my brother came of age to play ball sports, our household stayed busy with the extracurricular activities we were all involved in, such as softball, basketball, gymnastics, baton twirling, community swim team, tennis lessons, and piano lessons.

Whatever we wanted to do, my parents always supported us. We thanked GOD that we had two hardworking parents who could afford for us to be able to participate in everything we wanted to do. My parents were very involved and present parents as well. Our parents were always in attendance during every single practice, game, recital, meeting, etc. They were both always there for us, not only during the good times but also for the bad ones.

Chapter Two

When Jesus saw him lie, and knew that he had been now a long time in that case, he saith unto him, Wilt thou be made whole?

JOHN 5:6 (KJV)

For the next few years, life went on as usual. Then, in 1999, when I was 12 years old, my parents noticed a change in my behavior. I became very defiant and disobedient towards my parents. The behavior issues were not just confined to home, but they rolled over into school as well. I would talk back to my teachers, act out, be disruptive in class, bring inappropriate items to school, walk up and down the hallways without permission, etc. The worst thing of all, I became a bully to some of my classmates.

I stayed getting written up, and my parents stayed having to come to my school because of something I did. For the first time in my life, I did not care about getting into trouble or the consequences of my misbehavior. I definitely did not care about the punishment that followed. Everyone thought I was acting out or trying to fit in with my peers, the usual teenage angst. No one could have ever imagined it could be a medical condition until the following summer. While I was playing summer league softball, my parents noticed a change in my performance, stamina, attitude, and, most importantly, a change in my weight. I lost so much weight in a short period of time. I was always tired and constantly complained about how much pain I was in. I also started to develop a rash on my face. My parents soon realized something was seriously wrong. They scheduled an appointment, and after running many tests, they finally confirmed that I had a thyroid condition. I was then diagnosed with hyperthyroidism, which meant I had an overactive thyroid. This diagnosis was just the beginning of many medical problems I would have throughout my life.

After being diagnosed, the hospital referred me to a pediatric endocrinologist in Mobile, Alabama. He, in turn, diagnosed me with Graves' Disease: a malfunction in the body's immune system that releases abnormal antibodies that mimic thyroid-stimulating hormone, also known as TSH. I was treated with Radioactive Iodine (RAI) for my thyroid condition and continued to have regular bloodwork done to see if the treatment was effective. However, after a few months, there still seemed to be a problem with my platelet count.

During a regular check-up, my bloodwork showed that my platelet counts were dangerously low. A spinal tap procedure was done, and I underwent a platelet transfusion at the Women's/Children's Hospital in Mobile, Alabama. After the results of the spinal tap came back, I was diagnosed with Thrombotic Thrombocytopenic Purpura (TTP), which is a rare blood disorder where blood clots form in small blood vessels throughout the body. The clots can limit or block the flow of oxygen-rich blood to the body's organs, such as the brain, kidneys, and heart. As a result, serious health problems can develop. Platelets help with healing cuts and bruises on the skin. Without platelets, there is no healing, so bleeding problems can occur.

After my first transfusion, I was transported to Memorial Hospital in Gulfport, Mississippi. There, I was admitted and underwent my second platelet transfusion. Under the care of a different staff, the doctor informed my parents that there were still issues going on with my bloodwork. This period was such a hard time for my parents because they did not like to see their child going through all this at such a young age. They felt hopeless because there was nothing they could do except pray. However, when you think about it, that was the best thing they could have done for me. Pray for answers, pray for healing, and pray that I return to my old self.

After a few more months of doctor appointments, bloodwork, and testing, I was finally diagnosed with lupus. Lupus is an autoimmune disease where the body attacks itself. It is a chronic inflammatory disease that affects blood vessels, kidneys, joints, skin, and the nervous system. We finally had an answer. Lupus was the root of all my health problems. After my diagnosis, I underwent intensive treatment at Memorial Hospital

CHAPTER TWO

weekly until my health was finally under control. I still had to continue to get my platelets checked on a regular basis. I also had to continue taking different medicines daily as well. Doctors told me that my illness would be something I would have to live with because there was no cure. As long as I continued with my regular check-ups and medication, I could still live a normal life. While my parents were happy and thanking GOD that my health was finally under control and being monitored, I was happy and thanking GOD that I could finally get back to what I loved most... PLAYING BALL!

Chapter Three

He that walketh with wise men shall be wise: But a companion of fools shall be destroyed.

PROVERBS: 13:20 (KJV)

By this point in my life, I had learned to deal with whatever came my way—not knowing that GOD was only preparing me for worse things to come. I was doing well in school by keeping my grades up and doing well on the softball field and basketball court. By the summer of my 9th grade year, my softball career had taken off, and I already had college coaches looking at me.

I had even met a guy that summer. His name was Arthur, and he was a "bad boy." I knew my parents would not approve, so at the time, he was my "little secret" for a while. Eventually, "my little secret" would be on full display.

While we were dating, I did not have my own vehicle. So, I would ask to get my parents' car and lie to them about where I was going. I also found myself making my way to his house. I would even sneak out and go pick him up to joyride. I was really in love with him, or at least what I thought was love at that age. Eventually, my love and loyalty to him would be tested one Fall night. I had snuck out and picked him and one of his friends up. He drove without a license, and I rode with just a permit. We did not even get down the street when the police pulled us over. Arthur jumped in the back seat and told me to get in the driver's seat.

When the police approached the car, they asked for my and Arthur's friend's licenses. Arthur was on the floor in the back, so he was not seen at all. When I told the police all I had was a permit, he told both the friend and me to get out of the car and come to the back. At this time, Arthur had climbed back into the driver's seat while the policeman ran our names. Suddenly, Arthur let the window down and told me to get in. He said he was about to go. It was like he was tired of sitting there and had better things to do.

I was so scared and nervous when he said that because I knew he was serious. I told him no, and he said he was about to take off. I looked at his friend and asked if he was coming, and he shook his head no. I then made a "ride or die" decision and jumped in the backseat, closed the door, and told him to just go. I felt like this was just a dream. I could not believe I was running from the police at 15 years old. It was a fast, scary, and dangerous one-hour-long pursuit. We drove through apartment complexes, ran through stoplights, ran over stop signs, turned corners on two wheels, and even went airborne a few times. In the midst of everything, I began to pray that GOD would keep us safe, if nothing else. Finally, when we were able to get enough distance between us and the police, Arthur decided we should ditch the car and run on foot. The only thing was, he decided to park the car at his house. After hiding out in an abandoned car for a few hours, we finally decided to walk home. It took forever, and by the time I made it home, the sun was coming up, and I still had to get ready for school. I knew today was going to be a long day, but little did I know this was just the beginning of what was yet to come.

When my dad woke up and realized his truck was not outside, he reported his truck stolen. He was told that his vehicle had been in a police chase the night before, but the suspects had gotten away. When my dad told all of us what the police said, I kept my mouth shut and acted as if I was just as shocked as everyone else. It was not until I got to school that I felt like I was home-free. Boy, was I wrong. Eventually, I was checked out of school and was on my way to the police station. In my mind, I thought I was going to jail. My heart was racing, and my mind was thinking about running again.

Once again, I found myself praying, "It's me again, GOD. You answered my prayer earlier by keeping us safe. Now, can YOU please keep me out of jail?!"

Chapter Four

There are many plans in a man's heart, Nevertheless the Lord's counsel—that will stand.

PROVERBS 19:21 (NKJV)

I was put into the interrogation room with two detectives. They asked questions about the night before, and of course, I did not own up to anything at first. Then, they started pressuring me about my boyfriend and what was his name. I finally told them about his friend and left it there. I did not give up my boyfriend, and to my surprise, they ended up letting me go. *Thank You, GOD.*

My parents were beyond furious, and they forbade me from seeing Arthur. I was also grounded and was not allowed to play in any softball games until my dad said so. I followed the rules for a little while, but then, with the help of my friends, I got back in contact with Arthur, and we began to see each other secretly again. Also, my softball coach could not take another loss in an important tournament we were in at the time, so he asked my dad if I could play, and in return, I would have to do laps during practice as punishment. My dad agreed, and after sitting out for two games, I was back on the field.

As time passed, I eventually got in trouble again when my parents found out I was still talking to Arthur. What was so crazy was that I knew he was not the one for me. We were on two different paths in life, headed in two totally different directions. I do not know if what we had was a forbidden love (a love we had because someone told us we could not be together) or if it was true love. Whatever it was, I had no clue that what started off as him being my first real boyfriend would become a thorn in my side for another 12 years.

The year was 2003, and my sister was graduating. I was still on punishment, so I really did not care about her graduation, but I had to go. My cousin was on punishment at the time as well. So, because my parents had to watch her that night, she also came along. We were never really close, so it was no big deal. Once we started talking, we realized we had more in common than we thought.

After that night, it was on, and we became the best of friends. I eventually met her boyfriend, and she met mine. After a while, her boyfriend started to bring his cousin Tony around all the time. Tony and I built a friendship, which soon became something more. Tony ended up moving in with his cousin, and we eventually started seeing each other even more. He knew I had a boyfriend, but we just could not help what was happening between us. Regardless of what was happening, I was not leaving

CHAPTER FOUR

Arthur for Tony. At that time, only GOD could separate us. Soon, that would be the case.

One summer day in August of 2003, I received a frantic phone call from Arthur. He seemed very panicky, breathing like he had been running. He asked me where I was, and I told him I was playing ball in Oklahoma. I played on the All-Star team every summer, and we traveled all over. One thing I do know is that GOD saved me from pure destruction that day. If I had been in town when Arthur called, I would have gone to see about him. Plus, whatever he would have told me to do, I would have done it. GOD truly was looking out for me that day.

Realizing I wasn't in town, Arthur was surprised and very upset. I asked him if he was okay and what was going on. Instead of answering, he mumbled something and hung up in my face. I did not hear from him for the rest of the weekend. By the time I made it back home, I was determined to speak with him and get an understanding as to what that call was about. However, after several attempts, I was not able to get in contact with him. After a few days of still not hearing from him, I got the shock of my life.

My mom brought the newspaper to me and said, "Isn't this your little friend?"

I had no clue what she was talking about until I read the paper. Right there on the front page, the paper said that my boyfriend Arthur and two of his friends had robbed a restaurant at gunpoint, pistol-whipped someone for their getaway car, got caught, and were all now in jail.

At that time, I knew he was a bad boy and had a record, but I had no clue it was to this extent. I did not know what to think or how to feel. I was also not prepared to hear the punishment for this crime. He had received 15 years day for day. I could not believe it. I did not hear from him until a whole year later, and although he could not really go into details, he told me he would be out soon. He also asked me to wait for him. Even though I knew about the 15 years they had given him, and I was dating Tony then, I still wanted to believe Arthur when he said he would be out in just one more year. So, I did what he asked. I waited. While I was with Tony, my heart still belonged to Arthur.

While Arthur was in jail, we stayed in contact over the phone and through letters. As time passed and Arthur still would not tell me when he would be coming home, I realized he had lied and that I would not see him any time soon. I became distant, but I told him I would still be there for him. By then, my focus was on someone else.

Tony and I had stepped it up a notch and decided to make things official. Tony and I were together more times than not. To make things even better, we had the same exact birthday, but he was two years older than me. When I was a junior in high school, my mind was focused on what big college I would attend on a softball scholarship once I graduated. However, Tony had reservations because he did not want me to go far and

CHAPTER FOUR

risk losing me. This thought process was the first sign of being in an unhealthy relationship, but I ran straight through that stop sign.

Then, during a game, while I was playing shortstop, a runner was on first. The batter hit a ground ball to the infield, and I ran to cover second base and attempt to turn a double play. While throwing the ball to first base, the runner slid into my leg, and I felt this sharp pain in my left knee right after I released the ball. I fell to the ground as I yelled out in agony. Later, I was told my screams could be heard all the way up the hill where a baseball game was being played.

I did not know what happened at first, but I knew something was seriously wrong with my knee. As I limped off the field, I felt like my knee was dangling and hanging on by my skin. In my mind, I wanted to believe that all I would have to do was ice it down, wrap it up, and take a pain pill. I would just need to rest it and be ready for the next game. But as I looked at everyone's faces when being helped off the field, I knew by their expressions that my knee would need more than ice and a wrap to heal.

Chapter Five

Dearly beloved, avenge not yourselves, but rather give place unto wrath: for it is written, Vengeance is mine; I will repay, saith the Lord.

ROMANS 12:19 (KJV)

After the game, I could still drive home because the injury was only to my left knee. No one in my family was present for the game, which was very unusual. So, when I made it home, my parents were very upset with themselves for not being there. I was not upset with them at all. I just wanted to know the full extent of my injury.

The next day, my knee had swollen as big as a bowling ball. Even when I showed my basketball teammates and coach, they all were surprised and said it did not look good. After seeing how swollen it was, an MRI was scheduled for the same day as our next softball game. After it was over, the nurse came in and said she was not allowed to tell me the exact results and that I would have to wait for the doctor. But she did hint to me that it was not good. After being led into another room, the wait seemed like forever before the doctor

CHAPTER FIVE

came in to deliver the heartbreaking news. He said I had torn my anterior cruciate ligament (ACL), medial collateral ligament (MCL), posterior cruciate ligament (PCL), and meniscus cartilage, which was also known as an unhappy triad or "blown knee." After receiving this news, I was speechless for a few minutes. I did not know what to say or think. I finally asked the doctors if this was the end of my softball career.

The doctor was very surprised with the question, but I was very determined to play again. He then said the chances of me ever being 100% were very slim, and of course, my knee would never be as good as GOD made it. He also added that it would take a lot of work pre- and post-operation during therapy on my part. Then, he finally said it was possible that I could play again. That was all I needed to hear. After leaving the appointment, I told my mom to take me to the game so that I could break the news to my teammates and coaches. I knew this was not going to be easy.

I started physical therapy about a week after I got the results. I was told the injury was so bad that I needed therapy before the surgery to help with the recovery of my muscles after surgery. Even my therapist could not believe how bad my knee was. He said I had a football injury and was doubting my ability to play again. I knew then that I would have to prove many people wrong.

The surgery went well, and I went home the same day. I would have to get used to having a wrapped knee and a pain pump inside my knee, but I was determined and focused on my goal. Before long, I was off the pain meds and crutches. I still had to wear my knee brace and walked with a limp, but I was on my way to making a full recovery.

Then, one summer evening, on a day I was allowed to drive, I took my knee brace off and put it all the way in the back of my vehicle. As my friend Lauryn and I rode around, we came across some guys we did not necessarily know but had seen before — though there was one I had never seen before at all. We stopped to speak with them and asked if they had seen some guys we were looking for, and they said no. Then, they asked if they could ride with us. At first, I was skeptical because I did not know much about them. However, my friend said they were all cool and it would not be a problem. So, I took her word and unlocked the door for them to get in, not knowing I was intentionally allowing evil into my car. I had no clue that the night would end with me going to the hospital.

After only driving for about 15 to 20 minutes, the guy I did not know said he was bored and wanted us to take him back to where we picked them up from. Lauryn told him he would have to wait because we were already on the other side of town. That is when things went all the way left fast. He called her the "B" word and told her to shut the "F" up because he was not talking to her. They began to argue, and he continued to call her out her name. I finally spoke up and told him I would take him back because I wanted to get him out of my car.

CHAPTER FIVE

During the ride back, they continued arguing with one another, and I could not get back fast enough. I kept telling Lauryn to ignore him, but she would not listen. The argument between them kept intensifying the entire ride back. Finally turning into the apartment complex, the guy took his time getting out because he had a few more things to say to my friend. I told him to hurry up and get out, and that was when he pushed my head forward from the back seat.

As I waited for the other two to get out, I did not see the main guy standing by my open window. As I began to turn my head to see what he was doing, I felt a sudden pain on the left side of my face. It felt like I had just gotten hit in the eye with a baseball bat. All I could see was stars, and I realized I had just been sucker punched by this guy. He then opened my door, dragged me out of the car a few feet away, threw me on the ground, got on top of me, and began to beat me like I was a grown man.

I could not believe what was happening to me. I could not just get up and run away because of my knee. I was glad I took my brace off, or else he would have attacked my knee as well.

As I was screaming at the top of my lungs for him to stop, I glanced briefly at my supposedly best friend and saw her just standing there. My only hope of getting out of this situation, the one who got me into this situation, my best friend, was just standing by the car with the other two guys watching me get my face beat in. I had no more fight left in me, and at that moment, I felt defeated.

I stopped fighting, kicking, and screaming. Then, all of a sudden, he stopped punching me, and I did not think things could get any worse. I was wrong.

The next thing I knew, he put his hands around my neck and began to choke me. That was when I realized this man was trying to kill me. I started acting like I was passing out so that he would stop. It worked. He finally let go and got off of me. I just sprawled out there, looking up at the sky for a few minutes. I finally got the strength to get up and limp back to my car.

Lauryn put her hands over her mouth and said, "Oh my GOD!"

I could feel that my face was swollen, and I knew I was bleeding, but nothing could have prepared me for what I was about to see once I looked into the side mirror of my car. I did not even recognize myself because of the swelling. I actually had to touch my face just to be sure it really was me I was looking at.

Lauryn then insisted, "We need to go!"

I yelled back to her, "Do you see my face?!"

There was a young girl outside who had seen the entire thing. She asked if I wanted to come in and clean myself up. While I was there, I asked her if she knew the name of the guy who just tried to kill me. Initially, she was hesitant but eventually gave me his name. I finally had a name to give to the police. I then called the police and asked the girl what her address was, and she said she did not want to get involved. I would later learn that this guy terrorized the complex, and I was not the first female victim of his, nor would I be the last. That was the reason she did not want to get involved. She did not want to be his next victim.

After talking to the police and giving them my location, I called my dad to tell him what had just happened. At first, he thought it was just an argument and told me to get home. But when I told him the guy beat me to a pulp, he was there before I even hung up the phone. The look on my dad's face when he saw me was one of disbelief. I had never seen my dad so hurt, and then he became furious.

As the police were talking to me, my dad was asking who did it, where he was, where he lived, and that he wanted the guy picked up now. While the police were trying to calm my dad down, I became very dizzy and collapsed to the ground. The police then called the ambulance, and my dad went crazy. All I remember after that was praying that the injuries to my face would not be permanent.

Chapter Six

Let all bitterness, and wrath, and anger, and clamour, and evil speaking, be put away from you, with all malice: and be ye kind one to another, tenderhearted, forgiving one another, even as God for Christ's sake hath forgiven you.

EPHESIANS 4:31-32 (KJV)

After reaching the hospital, they rushed me right in to get an x-ray of my face and head. Despite a lot of bruising, swelling, cuts, and a concussion, I did not have any permanent damage and would be allowed to go home within a few hours after observation.

The last thing one of the nurses whispered in my ear was, "I hope you'll find and get the person who did this!"

Looking at myself, I could understand why she felt so strongly. My eye had swollen shut, and my face had swollen all over. Luckily, school was out for the summer, so I did not have to see anyone unless I wanted company. However, I denied any visitors who wanted to stop by and check on me. It took about a month for the swelling to go down completely. It also took about the same amount of time for my family to calm down. Everyone wanted revenge on the guy that did this to me. However, as much as I hated him at that time, my

CHAPTER SIX

mind was more on my "friend" who caused this whole situation to happen. While I was healing, I learned that she was telling everyone that she had nothing to do with what happened to me and that she did try to help. I was beyond furious. While everyone was plotting against my attacker, I was plotting against my ex-best friend. After a while, though, my heart became tired. Tired of holding onto anger, revenge, and hate. Being angry and unforgiving weighs on you, and after some time, it takes a toll on you. Not wanting that burden anymore, I finally did what I thought was impossible. After about two years, I finally forgave them both.

Afterward, I found out about all the pain he had caused others. Most of them were females he had beaten like me, and even his own mother was scared of him. I knew I would receive vengeance from GOD, and with that, I decided to let it go. I actually felt a feeling of relief once I gave it to GOD. Holding onto grudges wears you down, cripples your mind, and keeps you up at night. Forgiveness allows you to move on, let go of the weight, and look towards the future. Yes, I was finally free of that burden.

By the time my senior year came around, my face had completely healed, but I could not say the same for my knee. I had to sit out my entire senior slow pitch and half of my senior basketball season, which we won state in basketball that year (class of "05"). However, I was in full swing when fastpitch season came around. I was so happy I was back playing again. Giving up the sport was not an option if I had anything to do with it.

Although I had to face the truth that my knee would never be the same, I still left everything on the field every game. We had a fantastic season that year, but no ring. My high school graduation came and went, and I was still able to receive a softball scholarship to Mississippi Gulf Coast Community College - Perkinston Campus (MGCCC). On top of that, my boyfriend Tony and I were completely glued at the hip. So, he decided to enroll at MGCCC as well. It seemed like too much to outsiders, but to me, it was love. I was living life to the fullest.

It was the summer of 2005, and school had just started when Hurricane Katrina hit. Our house was within walking distance of the beach and was hit pretty badly. We had to live in a two-bedroom apartment for an entire year. Our house had to be gutted and reconstructed before we could move back in. Even though the living arrangements were very cramped, Christmas made up for everything that year.

I received the best gift ever: a car. Not just any car, but a Lexus. Can you picture a 17-year-old student with a Lexus in college? Well, I was that girl, and I made sure everyone knew it. I could not wait for Christmas break to be over so I could return to school and show off my new car. Everyone loved it and congratulated me on my new ride. That is everyone except for my boyfriend.

At the time, Tony did not have a car, and I kept a car the whole time he knew me. Sometimes two at a time.

CHAPTER SIX

He became very jealous that not only did I have a new car, but guys were noticing me as well. By the time the softball season began, I was happy with where my life was headed. My best friend Sharon from the 9th grade and I were not only playing ball together, but we were also roommates. My boyfriend and I were now on the same page. My grades were better than ever, and I was preparing to play on the next level. Unfortunately, as the saying goes, all good things must come to an end. Boy, they definitely did.

After having my Lexus for only three months, I loved my car more than I should have. My boyfriend warned me, but I thought he was just being jealous once again. One thing is sure: "The Lord giveth and the Lord taketh away." Warning always comes before destruction.

It was a late Friday night, and Tony had gotten us drinks and a room. The whole situation started off bad because, one, I was underage, and two, I had a game in the morning, which meant I was supposed to be in by curfew anyway. Yet, I was out with my boyfriend drinking. After a few drinks, his friend came by the room and asked if we could run him to McDonalds, just across the street. Of course, I said yes because I wanted to drive my Lexus again. After getting his food, I yelled out something to some guys who came out of the store, and of course, my boyfriend flipped out.

After getting into a heated argument, we got back into the car. I was drunk, mad, and just wanted to leave. I should have driven back across the street and laid down. Instead, I took a right and drove up the street. I turned the lights off and began to drive extremely fast. I was coming up on a car in front of me and planned to drive around it. But I overcorrected myself and drove up a hill and was headed straight into a telephone pole. It was not until the last minute that Tony reacted just in time by grabbing the wheel and allowing the car to fishtail and wrap around the telephone pole instead of us hitting it head-on.

By the time I realized what had happened, I was being dragged out the passenger door by my boyfriend and his friend because my door was jammed, and the hood of the car started smoking. I was freezing cold and hoped this was all a bad dream. A few minutes later, the police and ambulance arrived, and the dream theory went straight out the window. I was hit with the reality of the situation. I had totaled my car after only three months because I was drinking and driving. The outcome was one of the worst imaginable.

When the police finally questioned us, we all agreed to say that my boyfriend was driving and that we had a blowout. I had to call my parents, who were there in seconds. I told them I was okay, and they were happy that I did not have to go to the hospital. I also had to explain to my coach what happened. After that, I still left with Tony and his friend to return to the hotel room. We stayed up all night trying to figure out how to get around without a car. The next day, we had a game, but I could not play because of the bruises and how sore I was. I vowed never to drink and drive again.

After the accident, Tony and I started to have problems. He became even more obsessive and began to crowd me more than usual. My family also pointed some things out to me and told me that our relationship was very unhealthy. I agreed that something was wrong and decided we needed a break. When I talked with him over the phone about our situation, Tony basically went crazy.

He started screaming and crying over the phone, and I could barely hear what he was saying. I told him to calm down, but Tony was not having any part of it. He said he was walking to the road and planned to jump in front of the next car he saw. I did not believe him until I heard cars honking horns at him in the background. I was able to talk him back into the yard, but I could not talk him out of doing what he did next.

The next day at school, I was asked to speak with a teacher of mine who happened to teach Tony in high school. She told me something was wrong with Tony and that she thought I should take some time away from him because he was not mentally stable. I did not understand what she was hinting at until she said, "Have you seen his hand?" At that moment, I knew exactly what had happened.

After talking Tony out of the street and back into his yard, he asked me if we were back together. I told him I still needed time to think but would still be there for him. The next thing I heard was a loud crash and him hollering. I asked him what happened, and he said he punched out the car window in his yard. Initially, I did not know what to believe, but I told him we were back together to keep him from doing any more damage or making any more threats.

I also told Tony to promise me he would not cause any more harm to himself. He said he would not and that he was going to put ice on his hand. This injury was what the teacher was talking about. I thanked her for this information and set off to find my boyfriend.

I could not help but wonder: Lord, what have I gotten myself into?

Chapter Seven

For I know the thoughts that I think toward you, saith the LORD, thoughts of peace, and not of evil, to give you an expected end.

JEREMIAH 29:11 (KJV)

When I finally caught up to Tony, I noticed his hand was wrapped. I asked to see his hand, and as he unwrapped it, I noticed blood. I could not believe what I saw when he finally got it completely unwrapped. His hand was cut, swollen, and bruised. He had really punched out the car window with his fist. It was a lot to take in, but I did not want any more problems between us that might result in that again. We talked about the issue and told each other that things should never get this bad again.

After a long talk and apologizing to one another, I felt like things were back on track again. Not too long after the incident, Tony proposed to me. I was more than willing to say yes. I was so happy to be engaged to my high school sweetheart. However, I did not get the same excitement from my family and friends. It did not matter to us, though. We felt our love was all we needed. As time passed and my softball career continued to rise, Tony began to feel the pressure of losing me again. I started to see a change in him. He became more obsessive over me, clingier, and less concerned with my softball career. He only wanted to know if I had picked a date for our wedding. Up until that point, I had not really thought about the engagement as much because I did not want to get married and settle down anytime soon. Yes, I was happy about it, but I did not plan on making that commitment until after I was done with school.

After hearing this, Tony was not happy. He revealed to me that he was scared I would go to another college, leave him behind, and find someone new. My love for Tony at the time was so strong that I could not believe he thought I would just up and forget about him. It was a lot for me to think about.

So, my first year of college softball was coming to an end, and I was playing in the last game of my freshman year. We were losing, and we had two innings left to go. I finally got a base hit to right field; however, I was not fast and got thrown out at first base. Not only was that the last out of the inning, but I hit the base wrong and thought I hyperextended my knee. So, because it was the last game of the season, I did not tell my coach about my injury or the pain I was in. After the game, I just iced my knee down. I could walk and run on it, so I did not think it was severe enough to get checked.

It was not until the start of the next season that I felt like something was wrong. I practiced, lifted weights, ran, etc., as if nothing was wrong, but inside, the pain

CHAPTER SEVEN

was almost unbearable. I finally told the trainer and began to get shots in my knee. Still, the pain never went away, and my knee remained swollen.

I was finally told to get an MRI. Never in a million years did I expect to get the news I did. I tore my ACL, MCL, and meniscus again. Then, I was told I could never play college ball again on this knee. Just like that, my softball career was over.

I was more than hurt. I was devastated. It broke my heart to know that everything I had dreamed about and hoped for my future was gone. I cried long and hard before I finally accepted the news. Once again, I had to go through surgery and physical therapy for my knee. When I told my fiancé, I was shocked by his reaction. He said he was glad I could not play anymore because now I could not leave him.

Those words cut me deep. Tony knew how much I loved playing ball and my dream to play on the next level—so having him tell me that he was happy made my head spin. I started to look at him in another way, and what I began to see was scary. I started to spend less time with him but remained in contact. Eventually, things would come to a head, and our fairytale would soon be over.

Chapter Eight

Have not I commanded thee? Be strong and of a good courage; be not afraid, neither be thou dismayed: for the LORD thy God is with thee whithersoever thou goest.

JOSHUA 1:9 (KJV)

After my realization about my life partner, I started to rethink my future with Tony. I finally graduated from MGCCC. I was back to working and enrolled at USM, working on my bachelor's degree. I was more than done with him when he quit yet another job. After only a week, he decided he did not want to work there because of the pay. That was a complete slap in my face. While I was working two jobs, he did not want to work at all. I decided I had had enough and told him I needed a break. During our entire relationship, we consistently had breaks, and then we would make up.

However, this break was different for him and made him act in an unusual way. It started with about 100 calls a day because I would not answer. Then came the threats through text messages and voicemail. He threatened to kill all of my dogs and made threats towards my dad.

He also said, "If I can't have you, no one will."

After that, I noticed that one of my vehicles had been

CHAPTER EIGHT

keyed. I also almost got into a wreck on the way home from school one day because I thought my tire blew out in my other vehicle. After calling my cousin and upon further inspection, I soon realized that the cause of the blowout was my tire being slashed. I nearly got hit by an RV because my tire had been slashed. I did not want to believe it was him. It was not until about two years later that he admitted to stabbing my tire with a knife the night before it blew out. You would have thought this would be the end of it, but no, it was just the beginning.

Along with him vandalizing my cars, Tony would come to my job and just sit and watch me as I worked at the front desk. Every day, I would see him staring at me while he sat on the visitor's bench in the showroom. I soon had to get moved to the back and be escorted to my car every night because this was a constant problem. I also provided my job with pictures of him to be put up throughout the building because he was no longer allowed on the property. Someone even told me to get a restraining order on him. But without warning, all the harassment came to an abrupt stop one day, and I figured he got tired and had finally left me alone. Boy, was I ever wrong.

One day, while working in the back, where only employees were allowed access, I suddenly felt like someone was watching me. I turned around, and there he was, just standing there. I was frozen in place with fear in my heart. I honestly thought he was there to kill me. I did not know what to say or do at the time. As I looked him dead in his eyes, he began to talk, but I could not hear a word he was saying. I could only see his lips moving as I prepared for him to do whatever it was he came to do.

Fear had blocked my hearing, thought process, judgment, and apparently my motor skills cause I was unable to move a muscle. I asked myself how it got to that point. I could not help but wonder: Why is this the way I have to go? What will my parents think? And how in the hell did he get back here?

Finally, I heard him say, "I will always love you, and you do not have to worry about me anymore."

Then, Tony turned and walked away. I could not believe this was happening. I began to cry and had to walk outside to gain my composure. I went to my car, called my mom, and told her what had happened. She thanked GOD because that was all that happened. I also thanked GOD because I know it could have been the other way. He could have chosen violence against me, but instead, he had simply walked away. What made it crazier was that the restraining order papers were right there in the front seat, ready to be turned in.

A few weeks went by, and there was no sign of him. Even though nothing out of the ordinary was happening, I was still stressing over the fact that Tony could still be plotting his next move against me. Not only was that one of the issues I was dealing with at the time, but I also had one of the worst flare-ups in my life from lupus. I first started losing weight at a rapid speed, and then my

CHAPTER EIGHT

face began to swell. My eyes had swollen so badly that my eyelids had burst through the skin. My hair had also begun to fall out to the point that I had to start wearing wigs.

Then, one day at work, I collapsed and had a panic attack. I was rushed to the hospital and did not know what was going on with me. I could not return to work because I feared that something at work had triggered it. I went to the doctor, but no one could tell me what was going on with me. I had never experienced anything like this before. I finally got a call from my rheumatologist to get bloodwork done.

As I drove down the street, I felt dizzy and weak. I ran into the ditch and cracked my windshield. I was so out of it that I still tried to continue driving. Fortunately, my uncle was coming down the road when he saw the accident. He stopped me before I could drive off and called my dad to tell him what had happened. He said I did not look too good, and my dad instructed him to take me home. He also had my aunt come pick me up and take me to the hospital to get my bloodwork done.

As I returned home, I felt worse. Not too long after I got home, my dad came home and told me I needed to pack a bag to head back to the hospital. The results from my lab work had come back. I had contracted a staph infection on my upper left thigh, and because of my already weakened immune system, it had gotten out of control, which was the cause of all my health problems. I could not remember the trip to the hospital or most of what happened during the time I was there. I had a fever and was close to death because the infection had become sepsis.

The doctors could not understand why it took so long for the problem to be discovered. I had a mild operation done where they had to cut the infection out, and I was left with a big hole in my thigh. Then, they packed it with gauze, which was very painful. They also had to teach my parents how to pack and treat my wound because I was unable to do it due to the location. After a week in the hospital, I was finally allowed to go home on my 21st birthday. Man, what a birthday gift. Time goes by slowly when you are in the hospital. I was still very weak and fragile, but I was so thankful to be going home.

Only after about a week or two of being home did my parents realize that I was still losing weight and having problems. I had started losing my memory. I was dealing with awful insomnia, where I found myself staying up for three days straight. I was losing my hair. My eyes were still swollen and getting dark underneath. You would have thought that was it, but of course, it was not. Not too long after being released from the hospital, I started to develop boils all over my body. I even had to go to another wound care facility for treatment.

Once again, I had to go through the painful process of getting my wounds cleaned and packed once a week until they were all healed. I had about seven boils in different locations on my body. I had also contracted

CHAPTER EIGHT

shingles on the back of my neck and the side of my face. Along with everything else, I developed muscle weakness and a blood disorder (thrombocytopenia), and I had three more panic attacks. I had to sit out a year from school because I physically could not continue at that time due to my health.

None of this made sense to me. Jesus promised He would take care of me. I knew as a Christian, I would have to endure some things, but at that time in my life, I felt like giving up. I felt like I was too young to deal with so much at once. But Job 23:10 (KJV) says, "But He knows the way that I take: when He has tried me, I shall come forth as gold." So, I knew in due time, this would all be over, and I could move on with my life. The when was what I was waiting on.

Everyone had been praying for my family and me, and let me tell you, prayer works. After a year of doctor visits and hospital stays, I was finally improving. I realized I owed GOD the praise because of this milestone. I was already going to church before getting sick, but I still felt like I needed to do more. I owed GOD so much more of me. I continued going to church every chance I got. I was there every time the doors opened. I also started going to Sunday school and Bible study.

Eventually, I was asked to begin substituting when the teacher was out for Sunday school. I was more than happy to teach the children. Who knew I would be good at it? I was just glad to serve. But little did I know this was just the beginning. After half a year, I went from being a substitute teacher to a permanent teacher of the teenage girls' Sunday school class, a youth advisor, and singing in the choir. I still had to build up my energy, but I was healthy enough to return to school.

Then, on August 21, 2010, my sister finally got married, and I was so happy for her. She found "her person" in life. He was good to her and good for her. As I watched this beautiful matrimony, I started to think about my love life. I now had two examples, my father and now brother-in-law, of what kind of man I hoped to marry and the characteristics I wanted him to possess.

Even though this day set the stage for what kind of man I hoped to find, things did not go as planned in my relationships to come. I first ended up dating an ex-con, and after we cut all ties, I found out two years later he had killed his cousin because she had become pregnant with his child, and he did not want anyone to find out. Go figure. At that point, I just wanted to finish school and get my degree.

In August of 2011, I received my Bachelor of Psychology from William Carey. Praise GOD, I finally did it. I was officially a college graduate!

Chapter Nine

Be careful for nothing; but in every thing by prayer and supplication with thanksgiving let your requests be made known unto God. And the peace of God, which passeth all understanding, shall keep your hearts and minds through Christ Jesus.

PHILIPPIANS 4:6-7 (KJV)

A month after graduation, I applied for and was offered a job as a case manager. I was ecstatic about not only finding a job so soon but I would be working in my field of study and putting my degree to use. Things were going smoothly for me by this time, and I could not have been happier. I was in a relationship that was pretty much on its last leg, and I was ready to be done with the whole situation. I just wanted to be free to see what else was out there because that relationship was definitely for the birds.

This particular guy was the true definition of a "dirty dog." He cheated on me every chance he got and did not care that he was hurting me during the process. Later on in the relationship, he confessed that he just loved women. That was the reason for his lies and cheating. At this point, I told myself the streets could have him. I was trying to focus on my new job. But after only about two months of working, I was not getting the fulfillment in my work like I desired. I felt I was not helping anyone or making a difference. Besides visiting my clients for only 10 minutes and documenting what took place, nothing else was really required at my job. Not to mention, there was not much training provided for the position. I wanted to have more of a purpose in life and make a difference. Since I was dissatisfied with my current position, I decided to apply for another job in my field.

Not long after applying, I received a call to come interview for the case manager position. I was offered the job the day after the interview, and of course, I accepted the offer. Not only would I be making more money, but it was also closer to my home. This opportunity was perfect. After transitioning from one facility to another, I found my stride and realized that this was my calling. I finally understood the saying, "If you love what you do, it's not a job." This was my life, and I was made to help people and advocate for those who did not have a voice.

The joy I felt for making a difference in people's lives was fulfilling in my heart. I also reevaluated my life and often thanked GOD for the cards He dealt me. After seeing and hearing what most of my clients had gone through in their lives and the reason behind many of their problems, I felt that my life seemed like a cakewalk compared to theirs. Although I could not buy them happiness or, better yet, a fresh start in life, I could help them in other ways and, most importantly, help them get back and keep their children, which is GOD's most precious gift.

CHAPTER NINE

Although not all of my families were a success, I was happy that I was a voice for most and helped many get their cases closed out of the system so that they could move on with their lives. There is no better feeling than knowing that you changed not just one person but an entire family's life for the better. What made me so passionate about my position was the fact that because I had already been through a lot at a young age, I could relate and, therefore, empathize with most of them. I felt like GOD had me go through all I had been through for this moment.

Often times I would have a family where one or two of the family members were molested, raped, or sexually assaulted at some point in their lives. To hear this was devasting to me every time, no matter how many times I had heard it. I knew that coming into this field, I would hear some of the worst stories anyone could ever imagine. But never in a million years would I have ever thought that I myself would one day fall victim to rape!

Chapter Ten

Howbeit he would not hearken unto her voice: but, being stronger than she, forced her, and lay with her.

2 SAMUEL 13:14 (KJV)

One night, after riding home from the movies with a guy I had been dating, he suddenly pulled over in an empty parking lot. I asked him where he was going, and he just remained silent. He then parked behind the building and turned the car off. We sat in silence for about two minutes before he started kissing me. I was okay with that but was confused about why we had to come here for this. Suddenly, it became clear what he wanted, but I was not up for that, especially not here or like this.

The guy attempted to pull my dress up, and I told him no. He then reached over to my side to pull the latch on the seat, and I flew back since the seat had gone all the way back to the back seat. He climbed on top of me as he held my arms above my head with one hand and undid his pants with the other. I became very nervous and scared about what was happening and what would soon follow. After minutes of struggling, trying to get

CHAPTER TEN

him off of me, and screaming, telling him no, I soon became exhausted. He was twice my size, and I did not stand a chance against him.

During the struggle, he said nothing at all, but he was sweating profusely because of the fight I was putting up. Finally, he managed to lock my legs open with his legs and proceeded to sexually assault me right there in the front seat. I laid there frozen, quiet, and pissed that he had gotten exactly what he wanted. I asked myself, why me? He was someone I would have never expected this from. Once it was over, he climbed back into the driver's seat, and I slowly got myself together.

My thought process was, well, we had sex before, so this could not be rape, right? Even though I knew the answer, I did not want to believe it. He drove me home, and the only thing he said was goodnight. I went inside, took a shower, called two people I trusted at the time to tell them what happened, and I made them swear not to say a word. After that night, I promised I would never speak of this situation ever again. I did not want to think of myself as a victim. Nor did I want to believe a guy I was involved with was a rapist. So, I made up my mind that this was just my first rough sex encounter.

However, no matter what I thought or wanted, this topic would become very sensitive to me throughout the years. Thus, whenever my clients spoke to me about the subject, I could relate because of my deep, dark, hidden secret. The scene would replay in my head many times when the word came up. I was in denial for so long, trying to convince myself that he did not assault me. I could only tell myself that for so long before it got to the point where I could not even look at him without thinking of that night. We never spoke about it, and I never brought it up. Things became weird between the two of us, and we eventually cut ties not too long after. I could never look at him the same after that.

However, I refused to let that situation hinder me from moving forward in my life. As the song says, I shook it off and packed it under my feet. I washed my hands and threw in the towel on the dating scene. It was not for me. Time and time again, my sister would try to get me to talk to this guy and that guy, but I was not feeling any of them. Then, one day, she invited me to a party and said we would stop by her friend's house just to speak since he was not attending the party. She told the guy to come outside when we pulled up.

When the guy came outside, he looked in the car at me from her side of the car and said he needed a better look. So, he came to my side of the car and had me get out and do a spin for him. This action was very entertaining, considering the fact that he had not believed my sister when she told him she had a sister. He said goodbye, and we drove off. A few minutes later, her phone rang. She spoke a few words, and then she hung up.

My sister looked at me and said, "Craig is coming to the party."

Chapter Eleven

It was but a little that I passed from them, But I found him whom my soul loveth: I held him, and would not let him go,

SONG OF SOLOMON 3:4 (KJV)

In 2011, my sister worked the same job as Craig, so this was how she knew him. During that time, I was single and ready to mingle. My sister was always bragging about me at her job and how I would be a good catch for someone. Craig became curious as to why I was still single if I was such a good catch. He also had doubts as to whether or not my sister was exaggerating the truth. At first, he was hesitant, but he finally agreed to meet me and see if I was the real deal.

I already knew Craig from high school. He was a few years older than me, and he and my sister were in the same class. He knew her but had no clue I even existed. So, of course, he did not believe my sister until he saw me for the first time, and he was blown away. He told me how beautiful I was and decided to come out with my sister and I that night. We exchanged numbers and went from there. Neither one of us could have ever imagined that this would be the start of something so much more than we expected. You see, when Craig and I first started talking, everything was great. We spent much time together, spoke on the phone for hours, enjoyed each other's company, and, most importantly, got along very well. The only problem was that we had trust issues because of our past relationships. Neither one of us wanted to commit to one another because we were both afraid of getting hurt. At the same time, we wanted to be together but did not know how to express ourselves. So, we stayed "single" for a year while still dating one another.

What's crazy is how our minds get going, and it just has you thinking the worst in certain situations. This is why communication is crucial in relationships. How can your partner know what you want if you don't communicate your needs or desires to them? We both knew what we wanted but did not know how to say it. Well, eventually, we made it official on Memorial Day of 2012. Neither one of us really thought we would even get past a month, let alone a year. But we made it and were ready to start our new relationship.

Craig had a wonderful personality. He kept me laughing, and he always complimented me. We could talk about anything because he was so understanding and open-minded. We never ran out of conversation topics. He was always loving and caring and always let me know what a blessing I was to him. Regardless of his size, and yes, he was a big guy, he was and will forever be my big teddy bear. I always felt safe around him. It

CHAPTER ELEVEN

was like I had my own security guard.

When we met, Craig had a job, had his own car, and lived with his friend. I was cool with it because I was still living with my parents, trying to save money. So, everything was good. My family and friends initially liked him, mainly because I was also bragging about how he was such a good guy. Man, I wish I could turn back the hands of time because everything seemed to just go left one day.

It started off with the gambling. Craig had a bad gambling problem. At first, I thought nothing of it when he told me he was going to the casino. Then, I started going with him. I saw how much money was being thrown away. But the worst part about it was the simple fact that I went from never gambling a day of my life to becoming a frequent visitor at the casinos. Then, Craig lost his job and, eventually, his car. This misfortune was the start of his depression.

The crazy thing about it is that even though he did not have a job or car, the trips to the casino did not stop. If anything, we went more because Craig now had more time on his hands. Plus, I never said no—silly me. I eventually started to resent him because he introduced me to gambling and could not help me pay for anything. Hell, he could not even pay his own phone bill, and yes, I paid that too. If you ask me why I even stayed, it was because I loved him and wanted him happy, even if it meant my unhappiness. I still held out hope that we would hit it big at the casinos and everything would be fine. Yet, he still did not have a job or a car. I paid for everything and took care of him for the most part. I mean, he was my man, my responsibility, right?

By this time, Craig and I stayed getting into it. When we were not arguing, we were going somewhere in my car and spending out of my pocket, which made me mad all over again. Not to mention, he started to become possessive. He was so afraid of losing me. I was stuck between a rock and a hard place. Finally, one night, he made me so mad that I decided to get another guy's phone number out of anger, not thinking I would ever use it. I soon found out how wrong I was. The following week, he made me mad again, and I put the number to use. That's when Desmond came into the picture.

Now, Desmond was a very fun, energetic, attractive man. He made me feel so special. I was straight up with him and told him I had a boyfriend, but he did not care. Desmond was into me. He cooked for me, rubbed my feet after work, gave me money, took me out, and was basically doing everything Craig should have been doing. Desmond eventually became "boyfriend #2," and I did not see that coming. I got his number out of spite and ended up falling in love with another man. This went on for a few months until Craig became suspicious. I knew the lies and cheating would eventually catch up to me. The saying is true, "What goes on in the dark will come to light," and it definitely did.

One night, after Craig and I made it back to his mom's house after a night out drinking, I passed out on the

CHAPTER ELEVEN

bed. Craig took advantage of me being passed out and decided to go through my phone. I did not keep a lock on my phone at the time, so he was free to do whatever he wanted, and that he did. He read all the messages between Desmond and me, even the ones where we told each other we loved one another. I eventually woke up after some time and felt around for my phone under the pillow. My heart sank when I felt nothing but a cool sheet. I rose up and called for Craig, and he slowly came out of the bathroom with my phone in his hand.

The look of disappointment on Craig's face said it all. He knew everything. I asked for my phone, and he asked how I could do that to him. I told him I did not want to have that conversation at that moment, but he insisted. When I went to get my things, he grabbed me by my leg and drugged me across the bed. I managed to kick him, but then he grabbed me again and squeezed me tightly on both sides.

I started to yell, and he let me go. He then put the phone out for me to grab, only to trick me and throw me into the closet. By this point, his mom was yelling up the stairs, asking if everything was okay, and he said yes. I told him I was leaving, and he kept saying, "No." I knew it was my fault, but he pushed me to cheat. I just did not know how to leave. But everything was out now, and I was somewhat relieved.

When I tried to open the door again, Craig slammed it, and finally, his mom came up and asked what was going on. She asked me if he put his hands on me, and like a dummy, I said no. He explained to her that I had cheated and how badly he was hurting. I was apologizing as I was getting my things together. He was crying to his mom as she was telling him to let me go. I knew things were over between us. The sad thing about it was that I was not even bothered by the fact that he put his hands on me. I was sad that I had broken his heart.

Chapter Twelve

Love suffers long and is kind; love does not envy; love does not parade itself, is not puffed up; does not behave rudely, does not seek its own, is not provoked, thinks no evil; does not rejoice in iniquity, but rejoices in the truth; bears all things, believes all things, hopes all things, endures all things.

1 CORINTHIANS 13:4-7 (NKJV)

The very next day, I was with Desmond, updating him on last night's events. Desmond said regardless of what I did, Craig had no business putting his hands on me. It was not until this point that I realized how serious this was. Craig definitely put his hands on me, and I was more worried about his feelings last night. What was wrong with me? Never have I ever allowed something like that to happen. This situation was not something I would have ever thought would happen to me. Unbelievable!

Once again, Desmond was there for me, as always, doing what he did best. He was very compassionate and made me feel better over lunch. I went home and called one of my friends to tell her about what happened as well. While I was on the phone with my friend, my sister came into my room looking suspicious, but I did not think anything of it. I just wanted her to get whatever she came for and leave so I could get back to my story.

Little did I know she was outside my door listening in on everything with her nosy tail. So then, my sister decided to tell our dad, and now the cat was out of the bag.

Long story short, my family wanted blood: Craig's blood. Things continued to go from bad to worse for me. While Craig and I were on the outs, Desmond and I grew closer until he decided to drop a bomb on our relationship. He told me he was moving back to Ohio to be closer to his daughters. I could not be mad because I knew he had kids and would never want him to choose. But I needed him with me then, so it was a hard pill to swallow. On top of that, I was starting to miss Craig. To my surprise, he was missing me too.

While on vacation with my family, I received a text from Craig. It was a picture of me; underneath it, he said, "I miss you." That simple act moved me. I told him I was missing him too and that we would talk once I got back in town. Three weeks after the fight, Craig and I were back talking. I was not ready to see him just yet, but I did miss hearing his voice. We had to keep this a secret from everyone. More so for me because I was so embarrassed about this entire situation. But as the saying goes, "Love will make you do some crazy things." I guess I was a psycho!

And just when I thought things could not get any worse, I started to realize my stomach was larger than usual and that there was a hard lump right under my belly button. At first, I did not think anything of it. But as the days went on, it started to worry me. I went to the doctor, and the doctor informed me that I was either pregnant or had fibroids. I was speechless. Neither one of the outcomes was better than the other. While waiting at the doctor for the results from the ultrasound, I decided to text Craig and update him on what I had just been told.

Needless to say, Craig was more concerned for me than I was for myself. He first apologized for what happened between us and said that he should never have put his hands on me. Craig also said he was even more upset with himself for doing that while I could potentially be pregnant with his child. He felt so bad about possibly hurting the baby. While I appreciated his apology and concern, my mind was spinning about the potential what-ifs. There was so much to consider! But then, the time had come for the results. I was not pregnant but, in fact, full of fibroids. This result was better than being pregnant because although Craig and I were on good terms, we knew the good-term periods never lasted long. So, did we really need to bring a baby into this world together? Absolutely not.

After talking with my doctor about the different options, we agreed to start a medication that would help shrink the fibroids before we do anything else. However, after about two weeks, the fibroids did not shrink; instead, they grew larger in a short time frame. I went back to the doctor and discovered that the biggest one had doubled. She then went on to tell me that usually, when fibroids grow at a rapid speed like this, they are cancerous. I could not believe what I was hearing. I told my parents and my dad that I should get a second opinion. I was given the same results from another doctor and was told to have the surgery.

The surgery was scheduled for December 26, 2013, the day after Christmas. Thankfully, everything went well with the surgery, and the fibroids were sent off and were confirmed to be benign. Praise GOD! This was just another hurdle I had gotten over. About a month after my surgery, Desmond was all packed up and headed to Ohio. It was hard to see him go, but I knew the reason. We agreed to keep in contact, but our relationship was pretty much nonexistent after three months. Go figure.

On top of everything else, Craig and I had been discussing the possibility of seeing one another and getting back together. I did not know then that this would be one of the biggest mistakes I would ever make. Our relationship would soon become what one would say toxic! I could not complain because I had voluntarily put myself in this situation. But going back in was even worse than before.

Craig was no better off than he was when we broke up. He still had no job, car, or income and was back home with his mom. Basically, he had nothing going on for himself, and guess what? I still took him back. I never thought that this would be my life.

I was so stressed beyond my limits. My family had also discovered that Craig and I were back together. So, I was arguing with them as well. Life was stressing me

CHAPTER TWELVE

out, and things would not get better anytime soon. The arguing between my parents and me became so bad that they were ready for me to go.

One day, while I was at work, my mom began to text me and ask for my SS number, income, work information, etc. I did not have a clue what all this was about, but I trusted her, so it was not a big deal. Before my workday was over, I had a whole new address. My dad went and got me an apartment. I did not know whether I should laugh or cry. Great, another problem I did not need. My parents literally kicked me out. All I could hear was, "Hit the road, Jack!"

No one knew my finances, but Craig and I, and my finances were definitely shot to hell. So, no, an apartment was not what I needed at the time, but there I was with a new expense. However, after about a week of moving in, I was very excited about having my own place. It made me feel so much more independent. But, of course, happiness does not stay with me for too long. After being in my apartment for only three weeks, Craig had a serious health scare.

One morning, while I was in the living room doing my lesson, Craig came and sat with me. This act was very uncommon, but I was cool with it. He said he wanted to get out of the house, and I told him we could figure something out once I was done. All of a sudden, he grabbed his chest and fell to his knees. I asked him what was wrong, and he said he did not know but that his chest was hurting and that it was hard for him to breathe. I asked him if he wanted to call 911, and he said no. After watching him struggle to breathe for another minute, I decided just to put on clothes and take him to the hospital myself. At first, Craig did not want to go, but after some convincing, he finally agreed.

I raced to the hospital, running red lights like we were in the ambulance. As soon as we made it, they rushed Craig to the back due to his chest pains. They had him in the observation room well into the evening. He was up, talking and laughing, so we thought he would be released that night. We were mistaken. They told us they were going to admit him due to his blood pressure being extremely high. Although I was surprised since he seemed to be doing well, I just figured it was a precaution. So, I had no choice but to leave without him, expecting to pick him up the very next day. *Wrong again!*

Chapter Thirteen

Is any among you afflicted? let him pray. Is any merry? let him sing psalms. Is any sick among you? let him call for the elders of the church; and let them pray over him, anointing him with oil in the name of the Lord:

JAMES 5:13-14 (KJV)

I walked into the hospital asking about him, and all I can remember them saying was ICU. They led me to his room and pulled back the curtains. Seeing Craig unconscious and hooked up to so many different machines instantly brought tears to my eyes. It was rough on me to see him like that, but I was determined to do whatever I had to do to help with his recovery. Craig was in the hospital for an entire month. ICU for a week, then moved to a regular room for the next three weeks.

Once he was in a regular room, I stayed with him every night. I would wake up, put on my clothes, go to work, get off, go to my apartment, shower, eat, pack a bag, and head to the hospital just to do it all again the next day. Not to mention, I got up with Craig throughout the night when he had to go to the bathroom, so I did not get much sleep at all during that time. I could not even enjoy my new place because I was literally at the hospital the entire month with him. He asked me several times if I was going to leave him because he was so sick, and of course, I was not going anywhere. He needed me now more than ever. He was my man. How could I leave him now?

Finally, the day came for Craig to be released. We had planned for him to stay with his mom to give me a break finally, but of course, that is not what happened. He called me and said they were releasing him that afternoon, and he wanted me to come pick him up. I left work early to pick him up and take him back to my place. However, he did not stay long because we got into a huge argument only a few days later, and I called his mom to come get him.

At this point in my life, I was so tired. I loved this man with everything in me, but I was sick and tired of being sick and tired of him! With him back at his mom's, I could finally have some peace and start putting my life back together. I needed the break. I was going to take this time to really consider moving on, but my rollercoaster of life would not let that happen, and I got pulled right back into his life.

Only two weeks after our big fight, Craig posted that he was back in the hospital. I reached out to him, and he said he was having the same chest pains and breathing issues as before. He was admitted to the hospital yet again. We stayed in contact the whole week, and once he was released, he was right back at my place, and of course, we were right back together. This pattern was our relationship the whole year in my apartment. We would argue, break up, miss each other, get back together, and do it all over again. Some relationship, right?

HAPPY NEW YEAR 2016

I wanted to start the year on a good note between Craig and me. So, a few days into the year, I texted him while I was at work and told him we needed to talk. By the time I made it home, he was a ball of nerves trying to figure out what I wanted to talk about. I told him I wanted this to be "our year." Meaning I wanted us to get back to how things were when we first met. I wanted the arguing to stop. I wanted him to make things right with my dad since he always said we would get married one day.

And most importantly, I did not want us to go to bed mad at each other ever again. Craig agreed with everything, and we both agreed to make it our mission to keep these new goals we set for ourselves and our relationship. We were finally on the same page for the first time in a long time.

Not too long after this conversation, Craig got a call back from two different organizations about a position he had applied for and interviewed for. One of the places was at my job. We would have been working at the same facility. I was so happy because this had been a long time coming. Things were finally starting to look up for both of us. We were both happy that this was just the beginning of the year and things were already going in our favor. We had not argued in two weeks, and we got along so well that Craig stayed with me for two weeks straight. I had also started back reading, something I used to love to do all the time but stopped once Craig and I got together. It was almost as if I needed something to occupy my time. I wish I knew what was around the corner.

Chapter Fourteen

I saw a dream which made me afraid, and the thoughts upon my bed and the visions of my head troubled me.

DANIEL 4:5 (KJV)

I can't breathe! I can't breathe! Oh GOD, why can't I breathe?!"I began to gasp for air as I awoke from the horrible nightmare I was having. I glanced over at Craig; he was sound asleep, oblivious to what I had going on next to him. The CPAP machine helped with that. Oh, how I hated that loud machine. It was just a reminder of how sick he really was. But that machine is what kept him alive while he slept. Thank GOD, it was just a dream, though. No, it was more like a nightmare.

The second week into the year, I started having nightmares about someone dying. I saw myself asking GOD,"Why did you take him from me? Why did you do this?"

I was in tears in every dream, but I did not know who I was crying about because, at the time, there was no face. But what I was sure of was the fact that I loved this person dearly. What did this dream mean? This had never happened to me before, so I did not know how to feel. Besides, who wants to dream about people dying? Then, the scariest thing happened the following week.

I had the same dream, but this time there was a face, Craig's face! I saw myself posting his picture on my page, asking GOD those same questions:

"Why me?"

"Why did you take him from me?"

It was so real that once again, I woke up in a panic, crying and screaming. This time, Craig woke up with concern in his eyes. He asked me what was wrong, but there was no way I could tell him what my dream was about. He probably would have thought I was crazy. I actually thought I was going crazy because why are these my dreams? I started praying and rebuking the dream.

But it was all to no avail because little did I know at the time that this was not just nightmares I was having, but signs from GOD. First, He put it on my heart to have the conversation with Craig at the beginning of the year and then got me to start back reading. Finally, these horrible nightmares were interrupting my sleep. Yes, GOD was letting me know I should start preparing myself. For the worse!

Chapter Fifteen

In my Father's house are many mansions: if it were not so, I would have told you. I go to prepare a place for you. And if I go and prepare a place for you, I will come again, and receive you unto myself; that where I am, there ye may be also.

JOHN 14:2-3 (KJV)

On or around January 25, 2016, I developed two boils on my thigh. They were very juicy and painful. It was even hard for me to walk. As the days went by, they grew bigger and even more painful, letting me know they would pop at any given time. I told myself that if they popped and began to drain, there would be no way I could go to work the next day. But I did not know something even worse was brewing.

JANUARY 28, 2016

Sure enough, my boils popped the night before and were draining badly. So, I had to call in to work. Other than that, the day started off just like every other day. Craig decided he wanted to get a haircut and asked me to ride with him. I told him I did not feel like being out today because of my boils but that he could use my car. I decided to get myself something to eat and told him I would be right back. When I came back, I went straight to my room.

Craig walked in right behind me, and his last words to me were, "Okay, babe, I'm gone!"

I said, "Okay, have fun!"

I remember it like it was yesterday. Craig had on the bubble jacket I had gotten him for Christmas. He loved that jacket and wore it every time he left the house. A few seconds after we said our goodbyes, I heard something drop in the living room. I stopped chewing and said to myself that he did not just drop the brand-new television I had just gotten. But after hearing what sounded like someone running their nails over a chalkboard, I had to investigate. Nothing, and I mean nothing, could have prepared me for what I was about to see: Craig, my man, my best friend, the love of my life, was lying face down, gasping for air.

I yelled out, "Baby, what's wrong?" No answer!

Then, I ran back into my room to get my phone and dialed 911. After telling the operator what was going on, she then told me to roll him over on his back. Lord, why did she have me do that?

This image will forever be engraved in my memory. Craig was a sky-blue color. His face was so swollen that one of his eyes was about to pop out of his head, and the other was swollen shut. He had saliva running down the side of his mouth, and I just became hysterical. At that very moment, I knew I was going to lose him. The operator finally got my attention again and told me to

CHAPTER FIFTEEN

tell her every time he took a breath.

1, 2, 3, 4... Breathe.
1, 2, 3, 4, 5... Breathe.
1, 2, 3, 4, 5, 6... Breathe.
1, 2, 3, 4, 5, 6, 7... Breathe.
1, 2, 3, 4, 5, 6, 7, 8... Nothing.

"He's not breathing! OH MY GOD, HE STOPPED BREATHING!!!" I screamed.

As I'm grabbing at his shoulders with his head in my lap, my life as I knew it would never be the same. At that very moment, as I witnessed my boyfriend transition to the other side, a piece of me died with him. I HURT! An indescribable pain shot through my body and punctured my soul. I HURT! I had never felt a pain like this before. No pain would ever be able to compare. I HURT! My agony reached depths that I could not describe. I, Brittnei Michelle Farmer, was hurting, and there was nothing anyone could do about it.

It took the paramedics what seemed like forever for them to get there. They said they could not find the apartment number, so I had to leave Craig's side to meet them downstairs. I did not quite understand why it seemed as if everyone and everything was moving in slow motion. Even as I tried dialing his mother's number, my fingers were just stuck. They tried working on him in my living room for about 20 minutes.

Every time they shocked him with the defibrillator, I kept asking, "Is he breathing?"

I never got a response.

When they finally decided to take him out of the apartment, the urgency was gone. They were not rushing, nor was there much conversation between the paramedics. I knew he was gone. But yet and still, I held out a little hope that a miracle would happen or that I could finally wake up from this horrible nightmare. But when I attempted to get in the back of the ambulance with him, the little bit of my heart that held out any hope that they could save him burned out when they denied me access. He was gone. My future husband had passed away.

How could this happen? Why did this happen? Why could it not have been me going to heaven? Why was I left with this burden to carry? So many questions. There was no one to answer any of them.

As soon as I walked into the hospital and asked about Craig, I was told to go straight to the chapel. Before I even reached the room, his sister walked through the sliding doors. I looked at her with pain in my eyes, and she looked at me with hatred in hers. Oh Lord, I did not need this right now. So, I walked into the chapel without saying a word. Not too long after, the room started filling up. I do not quite remember who all came in or out. But I do remember his mother being there. She did not say much, and neither did I.

After a while, the coroner came in, and as we all stood to hear the news we dreaded, he finally announced that Craig was officially dead. I did not scream, nor did

CHAPTER FIFTEEN

I cry. I already knew. I was just in shock because this meant that it was real. Official cause of death: "Massive Heart Attack."

I sat down and just looked at the floor, replaying the night events and the conversation we had around New Year's about our future. I was even replaying the dreams I had two weeks ago and the one from just last week. Everything and nothing were adding up. This reality could not be my life right now. I could not come to terms with anything happening at that moment.

Then, out of nowhere, his sister accused me of his death. What is crazy is that even though that comment really pissed me off to the point that I wanted to attack her, not with my hands, but with my words, I could not do it. I was more hurt than pissed. More drained than energized. More dead than alive at that point. I almost wanted to say, "You can have it. I have nothing left inside. Yeah, you can have it."

So, instead, I looked at his mother and asked her to have an autopsy done. She said she would not do that because she believed the coroner. However, she asked me if we had argued that morning, and I told her we had not argued since our conversation. Craig had been staying with me for the past two weeks because things between us had been so peaceful lately. GOD had been speaking to me and preparing me for this moment, and I still would not have been ready for this test.

We were finally allowed to go back to see him. Craig was lying on the metal table as if he were just sleeping.

His face had gone down, and he just looked normal. There was no way he was gone. I had to sit down because my brain could not process what was happening. At the same time, my sister had texted me to let me know she had made it to the hospital. I do not even remember calling her and letting her know anything, but I was thankful she was there. I finally returned to the chapel, where I met my sister and my best friend Sharon. As soon as I sat down, I broke down. It was hard. I could not talk. I could not think. I could barely even breathe. Everything was just hard.

We walked outside, and I remember the sun was shining so brightly. I vividly remember this detail because I was mad about it being so pretty outside on this sad day. Now, I understand that the Heavens had opened up to welcome Craig into the Kingdom and that the angels were rejoicing. It was a beautiful day, but my insides were so ugly.

When I made it to my parents' house, I realized the back of my pant leg was soaking wet from my boils draining. I had forgotten all about them. By the time I took a shower and treated my leg, news had spread, and my phone was going crazy. I finally posted precisely what my dream said I would.

"Lord, why did You take him from me?"

Yes, exactly the same. The only difference was this was real life. This was real pain. I felt like I was moving in slow motion. I do not remember who called or who

CHAPTER FIFTEEN

came by. I just remembered I really did not want to be bothered.

Everything was a blur the next few days. I was in shock and felt like I was on autopilot. I had to go to the doctor and was put on anxiety medicine. I kept myself doped up to numb the pain. I stayed crying, I stayed hurting, and I stayed confused. I eventually returned to work after a few days, and even that was hard. Then, it was time for his funeral. To see him in that casket almost took me out again. I still could not believe this was real life. Craig was really gone. No more talks, laughs, or arguing. He was just gone. I was physically there, but mentally, my mind was stuck on what I could have done differently.

Just a few days after Craig's passing, I started having survivor's guilt. Not to mention, what his sister said to me kept replaying in my head. Did the arguing kill him? If so, why did I not go right along with him? I felt so bad that I was still here and he was not. Why was I spared? At the funeral, these feelings became extremely strong. I almost lost it when a picture of him and me appeared on the big screen. This is all I have left now: memories. I had a long road ahead of me.

You're Not Alone

Have you ever had a feeling
Like GOD wasn't there?
When you cry alone at night,
you wonder if He even cares.

Or maybe GOD seems distant,
too far to answer your call.
He may be too busy
to catch you when you fall.

So, you pray a special prayer,
asking GOD for a sign.
And just when you're about to lose hope,
He answers right on time.

Yes, I've felt this way
more than a time or two.
And what GOD has done for me,
He can do the same for you.

He holds every one of our tears
in a jar to keep,
when we're sad, lonely, or down,
He knows every time we weep.

YOU'RE NOT ALONE

He knows about our pain
and every problem our way
But they don't compare to the blessings
that are new each and every day.

Have you ever taken the time
to count your blessings one by one?
The greatest blessing of all
was when Jesus fought death and won.

Because He lives
I can face tomorrow
And even when I'm sad,
He gives me joy in sorrow.

Jesus was innocent.
Yet, my life was spared.
My guilt and disobedience,
they were my sins He bared.

Could they have been more cruel?
Hurting Him for what I've done.
Going from judgment hall to judgment hall,
the punishment had just begun.

They mocked, whipped, and teased Him,
trying to make Him feel shame.
They did all of this to my Savior
when He wasn't the One to blame.

The same hands I'm holding onto
are the ones that carried the Cross.
Those hands have a permanent scar
so that I wouldn't be lost.

GOD IS KEEPING ME

I'm sure Jesus asked the question,
"Father, are You even there?"
GOD answered Him and said,
"Son, I'm not going anywhere."

To see His only Son
Being bruised for my iniquity.
Then, allowing me to sing the song,
"Lord, I need thee!"

So, when you get discouraged,
on Him your burdens you cast.
You're just going through a storm.
Don't worry, it'll soon pass.

Whenever Satan attacks,
remember that day on Calvary.
Just call on the name of the Lord.
And the devil will have to flee.

You're stronger than you think,
so claim victory over anything.
You have the power to do this
because you're a child of the King.

So, the next time you feel like
your burdens are too hard to bear,
remember Jesus said, "I'll never leave you,"
and that He'll always be there...

Chapter Sixteen

The LORD also will be a refuge for the oppressed, A refuge in times of trouble.

PSALM 9:9 (KJV)

As the days went by, I felt myself become more and more depressed. I even stopped going to church. I only went to work and back home. I could not even do my job at work anymore. I was in the wrong mental space to function. I went to my supervisor and told her I did not know if I could continue my job duties anymore. How could I help these families when I could not even help myself?

My supervisor told me she did not want to let me go and asked how she could help. I told her to give me a few days to see if I could figure something out. Luckily, my coworker/partner felt my pain and stepped up. He told me I did not have to do anything except ride with him to our appointments and take notes. He said he would lead every visit, and he even did both of our parts. I was so thankful for him.

Although I was able to get that situation figured out, for the time being, my depression was at an all-time high. I also started to have nightmares and night terrors just about every night. January 28, 2016, kept replaying over and over every night. I could not eat, I could not sleep, nor could I even function correctly. I also started to see and hear things at night, like his CPAP machine. I did not know if it was all in my head or if I was really going crazy. I even started to feel him rub on my back, which made me jump out of my skin the first time it happened.

My job eventually told me about free therapy sessions offered through my insurance. I started going to therapy and was diagnosed with severe depression, severe anxiety, and PTSD. I was also put on other medications to help with the symptoms. I poured my heart out every time, but I was still not getting any better. Once my free therapy sessions ran out, I was once again left with my own thoughts, and what I was thinking was horrible. One day, I decided to just end the pain.

It's funny that once you come to terms with making this permanent decision, it seems like all your burdens somehow disappear. My whole mood changed, and for the first time since Craig passed, I was actually feeling happy. I went to three different stores and got over-the-counter sleeping medicine. I waited until my parents were asleep and poured all the bottles on the table. I also got a handful of my mom's Ambien and threw that in the mix as well. I put the pills into one bottle and just started taking them by the handful. They began to take effect almost immediately.

CHAPTER SIXTEEN

I could barely keep my head up. I closed the pill bottle and walked to my bed. I could feel my heart racing. I lay down and started thinking about who would find me in the morning. I knew I was dying. People say before you die, your life flashes before your very eyes. That was not the case with me. I just wanted the process to speed up instead of taking its time.

The feeling started in my feet. My muscles became weak. I had to tell myself to lift my leg. Then, I was not even able to do that at all. It kept moving up my body. I lost control of my bladder and felt myself wet the bed. As the weakness and numbness continued up my body, it finally got to my chest, and I could hear my heart pounding through my chest. It felt like my heart was going to bust. I thought to myself, if I had a heart attack, would it hurt?

Soon, I was unable to even lift my head. My body became so heavy it felt like I started to sink into the bed. The feeling finally made it to my head, and at this point, I had to remind myself to take breaths. Everything began to slow down, and I knew it would not be long before it was all over.

At some point, I felt bad because I knew my parents would find me and be heartbroken. But I had to go through with this. I finally began having trouble keeping my eyes open. They began to flutter on their own. Finally, they just became small slits, and all I could see was a bright, straight line. I said to myself, "It's time."

Then, I let go into complete darkness...

Chapter Seventeen

He has led me and made me walk in darkness and not in light. Surely He has turned His hand against me time and time again throughout the day.

LAMENTATIONS 3:2-3 (NKJV)

"Brittnei! Brittnei! Brittnei!" All I could hear was my dad yelling my name and telling me to get up. As my eyes fluttered open, it took me a minute to gather my thoughts because I definitely woke up dazed and confused. My dad asked me if I was going to work, and I told him I was not. He walked out of the room, and as I lay there, I finally realized I was still alive!

WHAT?! HOW?! WHY?!

I could not believe I made it through the night. I looked around the room, and everything was blurry. I thought I had messed up my eyesight. I felt around for my phone to call my job and let them know I was not coming in. I could barely see the numbers on the phone because everything was so blurry. I recalled that I had spoken with my supervisor the day before, so I just went to my call log to make it easier. Although I could not see the numbers, I could see when the phone scrolled

CHAPTER SEVENTEEN

down to a name programmed in my phone. When she answered, I was shocked that I dialed the correct number. As I began talking, I realized I also messed up my voice box. My voice was deep and raspy as I explained to her I was not feeling well and would be out for the day. Thankfully, she did not ask any questions and just said she understood, and we ended the call. I just laid there and asked myself, how am I going to go on with my life now if I could barely see or speak?

I got out of bed, and as soon as I tried to stand up, I fell to the floor. My legs were still asleep. The pills were still in my system. I used the dresser to help me up off the floor. Then, I used the door handles and wall to help me to the bathroom. When I finally made it to the toilet, I peed for about three minutes straight. I had so much fluid in my system from all of the sleeping pills.

I finished up and then headed to my dad's bedroom using the same technique I used to get to the bathroom. When I finally made it, I could barely stand. When my dad saw me, he reached out and grabbed me before I fell back. He thought I was having a panic attack, but I could not tell him what was really going on. He managed to calm me down after a while, and then we headed to my apartment.

Upon entering, it felt so cold. I was back where my boyfriend took his last breath. It seemed so unreal. I looked around as if someone was going to jump out and get me. I never wanted to return, but I had to move my things out. My dad fixed a few things around the apartment while I packed a few bags, and then we left. I could not be there too long, or I would have undoubtedly had a panic attack. I had the rest of the month to get the rest of my things out.

Throughout the month, I would go there alone to just lay in the very same spot Craig laid and prayed for GOD to take me away. He never did. I never told anyone this. I mean, I did not want anyone to think I was crazy. By this time, I knew I had completely lost my mind, and things were only going to get worse. Finally, the day came when I had completely moved out, and I could not be happier turning in my keys. Good riddance. After that day, I could no longer drive past the apartment complex without crying. This was hard, and the worst part about it was that I had to go through it alone.

During this time, my best friend Sharon found out she was pregnant and wanted me to be the godmother—finally, some good news. However, the excitement was only temporary, and the thought of losing my boyfriend crept back to the front of my mind. Try to imagine not only losing a loved one but being the only person there when they cross over. Not to mention the way he was looking while gasping for air. Now, put that scene on repeat. That is what I had to deal with on a daily.

One day, I woke up with a different approach to how I was going to take my own life. Instead of pills, I decided to do carbon monoxide poisoning. I started off by taking half a bottle of Xanax. Then, I closed my car up in the garage and put duct tape on all the openings. I

CHAPTER SEVENTEEN

got in my car and turned it on. I looked at the clock and closed my eyes. Then, out of nowhere, I heard someone scream my name, "Brittnei!" I jumped up, looked around, and did not see anyone. I looked at the clock and realized an hour and 20 min had passed. Wow! Once again, I am still alive. All I could think was, "Why?" After another failed suicide attempt, I became desperate to leave this earth. I decided to do suicide by cop. I got dressed in a black turtleneck pulled up over my face, a black hoodie, sweatpants, tennis shoes, gloves, and shades. *Yep, I was ready to set it off. Literally!*

Chapter Eighteen

Then He said to the disciples, "It is impossible that no offenses should come, but woe to him through whom they do come!"

LUKE 17:1 (NKJV)

I drove straight to the bank, figuring bank robbery was one of the best ways to commit suicide by cop. My mind was made up, and the Xanax helped me to remain focused on the task at hand. I was not scared of anything. I was actually pretty calm. I parked my car by a school close to the bank and got out. I walked around the side of the bank and through the front door, ready to carry out my mission.

The scene that plays out in movies was not like the scene right before me. It was not chaotic or anything. No one was screaming or running around. Everyone was just focused on me and my directions. My weapon of choice was two large chef knives because I have never been a fan of guns. Besides, I was not planning on hurting anyone, just myself. As I walked up to one of the tellers, everything seemed to be going in slow motion. I simply put the garbage bag on the counter and said, "Give me the money!" Calm, cool, and collected. You

CHAPTER EIGHTEEN

would have thought I had done this before because of how relaxed I was.

As soon as those words came out of my mouth, money was thrown into my bag. Wow! Just like that. I moved from one teller to the next. I was only in the bank for no more than 6-7 minutes before I grabbed everything, threw it all in the bag, and ran out. By the time I made it back to my car, I was totally out of breath. I took a second to catch my breath, but then the phone rang, but it was not my phone. I found myself thinking, "Whose phone did I grab? Oh no!" I threw that phone out the window and drove off.

I took the highway back to my house so that I could pass the bank on the left. There were so many police cars at the bank, but they just missed me by a few minutes. It only took 5 minutes to get back home, and still, I felt nothing. The Xanax was definitely doing its job. I was still high and unfazed to the point where I just threw the bag in my closet and got dressed for work. I did not think anything about it. On my way to work, I went through a roadblock. I asked what was happening, and the cop said someone had just robbed a bank.

I nonchalantly said, "Oh wow!"

They asked to check my trunk, and I obliged. They checked my trunk, thanked me, and told me to have a nice day. I went on to work only to get there and go straight to sleep. On the way home, I went through another roadblock. Of course, they were still looking for the "bank robber." The cop told me to roll my window all the way down, took one look at me, and told me to have a nice night. I guess I did not look like someone who would rob a bank. I went home, took a shower, and went back to sleep.

The next day, I had to go to a birthday party. I eventually drug myself out of bed after another long night of restlessness and nightmares. I went to the closet to find something to wear, and there, off to the side, was the black trash bag. I looked inside to see bills. Suddenly, I became light-headed after everything from the previous day flooded my brain. I was so high yesterday that I could not process anything until my high wore off.

Now that I was completely clear-minded, I began to panic. What if someone saw me? What if someone recognized me? Was it on the news? At the time, I could not think about it because I did not want to admit to myself that I had robbed a bank and actually got away with it. Or did I? It was eventually shown on the news, but my coverup was so good I did not even recognize myself.

As time passed, the thought played over and over in my head. Carrying this secret began to weigh on me. I decided to take a chance and tell someone. At the time, I was preparing for Sharon's baby shower. I was hosting it and wanted to take care of everything for her since I wanted that day to be special. We were best friends. She was like a sister to me. In my mind, Sharon was the perfect person to tell about what happened. So, I decided to tell her on the day we met to discuss plans and ideas.

CHAPTER EIGHTEEN

When I told her about what I had done, she was quiet at first and then said she did not believe me. Once I showed her pictures on my phone, she just looked like she was in shock. I thought to myself that I should not have told her, but I needed to tell someone. Since she was my best friend, I thought I could unload on her without worry. I honestly did not know what to expect or what the outcome would be.

However, I definitely did not expect the phone call I got from her the following day while I was at work. Sharon said she could not sleep at all the night before because of what I told her. She mentioned that it bothered her so bad it made her stomach hurt. I apologized to her and said I did not mean to stress her or the baby out. But then she said she was thinking about calling the police and turning me in. Her words hit me hard, and I was ready to fight her. I could not believe she said that to me!

My eyes got so big, and my mouth became so dry I could barely even speak, and I became extremely hot. I knew my blood pressure was through the roof. I walked out of my office and outside to my car. I wanted to curse her so badly, but I had to remain calm. I would have never thought my best friend would even think about sending me to jail. Was this really happening right now?

I had to think fast and come up with something to tell her so she would not dare call the police on me. I kept telling her it was a lie and that I was only thinking about robbing a bank. I do not know if she believed it, but we soon ended the call. I told myself I had to deal with yet another problem on my own. I guess you really can see who helps you push when the wheels fall off, and I was pushing this car all by myself.

About a week later, we still had tension, but I was hosting her baby shower like nothing was wrong. Despite everything going on, I still wanted this day to be memorable for her. Everything turned out better than I expected, and everyone seemed to have a great time. At the very end, my "best friend" handed me a note and told me not to read it until I got home. After cleaning up and loading up my car, I headed home. No goodbye or anything. I could only imagine what was in the letter, but I kind of had a feeling what it was about. Still, I was very eager to see what she wrote. Tears filled my eyes almost immediately.

My so-called best friend not only took the title of me being the godmother away, but she also did not want me in the birthing room when she delivered the baby, nor did she even want to be friends anymore. Just like that, my best friend, my sister, my ace, was no longer any of those. I felt oddly cold, hurt, and angry. She waited to give me this letter after the shower, after I paid for everything and put my all into that shower. Suddenly, everything I had done for her, covered up and kept secret, flooded my memory. Fortunately for her, I am not the type of person to get mad and start telling people's business. I will take all that to the grave. I brushed it off because I realized she was never a real friend. I will take that L and keep moving like I have been doing. Without her!

Chapter Nineteen

The LORD is nigh unto them that are of a broken heart; And saveth such as be of a contrite spirit. Many are the afflictions of the righteous: But the LORD delivereth him out of them all.

PSALM 34:18-19 (KJV)

By the time July rolled around, I was a complete mess. I was paranoid, and my anxiety and depression were at an all-time high. My nightmares and night terrors were worse than they had ever been. My insomnia had become to be my best friend. Then, to top it off, Craig's birthday was coming up.

The therapy sessions were a complete joke to me, with the therapist crying at every one of my visits. The medication I was prescribed made me feel high and out of it all the time, and I knew his birthday was going to be hard for me. His friends and I gathered at the beach for a balloon release. I do not remember much because I was drunk and high on my anxiety pills. I just wanted to numb the pain. I could only imagine how crazy I looked out there, walking, talking, and crying about Craig. I'm sure it was a sight to see.

Later that day, I came home and just sat in my room thinking. Everything that transpired was swirling around in my mind, and I was getting lost in the spiral when suddenly something broke me from my descent. Out of nowhere, I received a call from Desmond, the guy I cheated on Craig with, which caused Craig to put his hands on me. We had always been cool but lost contact when he moved back to Ohio. I never thought I would talk to Desmond again.

Talking to Desmond helped some, but the pain never went away. He was sad to hear about my boyfriend and sorry about what I was going through. He told me he was there for me and to let him know if I needed anything. Although he lived in Ohio at the time, I still wanted to believe everything he said to me. At the time, I felt like I had no one else. So, whatever I could get at the time, I held onto it.

Not too long after Craig's birthday, I received a call that my ex-best friend Sharon had given birth and was having complications. She had emergency surgery to have her gallbladder removed. I contemplated whether or not I would go to visit her, but eventually decided I would as this was serious. I put our issues to the side and had another so-called "friend" ride with me to New Orleans to visit her in the hospital.

On the way there, my transmission went out, which made the trip even longer. I called my dad, but he did not answer, so I just kept driving until we reached the hospital. The visit was very quiet and awkward. We both knew we had not spoken since I received that letter, and things were still unsettled between us. However, I still

CHAPTER NINETEEN

did not like seeing her like that. Despite everything, she was someone I had shared a connection with, and her being unwell did not bring me any pleasure. So, I kept things civil without showing just how wrong things were between us. Besides, I had other things to worry about.

Not too long after arriving, my dad finally returned my call. I told him about my car, and he yelled at me and told me to get home as soon as possible. I do not know why that upset me so much, but it did. I told Sharon that I would be praying for her healing, wished her well, and was out the door and back on the road home. It took about three and a half hours to get home because of my transmission. My dad yelled at me again as soon as I walked in the door. I just went to my room and started plotting. I was so furious. I felt like the walls were closing in on me and that my world was crumbling. This was the last straw. I had to get out of here.

Not only was I being yelled at like a kid, but everything reminded me of Craig. I could even still smell him. I finally made a call to Desmond in Ohio and took him up on his offer. He said, "*If you needed anything,*" right? I told him I needed to get out of Mississippi and asked if I could stay with him. Without hesitation, he said sure. I packed my bags, and at about 3:30 am, I loaded my mom's car with all my belongings. I was not planning on coming back. I put the address in my phone and set off for this cross-country adventure. GPS said 12 hours. I did not bat an eye. *Ohio, here I come!*

Chapter Twenty

And it came to pass, when the sun did arise, that God prepared a vehement east wind; and the sun beat upon the head of Jonah, that he fainted, and wished in himself to die, and said, It is better for me to die than to live.

JONAH 4:8 (KJV)

The drive was great. There was nothing but me and my thoughts. It was surprisingly peaceful. I only stopped three times: once for gas, once for food, and once for a potty break. Other than that, I was on the road. When I finally reached Desmond's house, he stood in disbelief on the corner. He did not believe me when I said I was really coming. Of course, he did not know my mental state either. As soon as I exited the car, I felt a strong sense of relief. I felt better for some reason. In my mind, this was going to be the fresh start that I so desperately needed.

We got all of my belongings out of the car and headed inside. We both knew this would be a big change for us, but we were willing to make it work because we were comfortable with one another. For now, anyway. We rode around so Desmond could show me his city and got something to eat. We even talked about going to get my address changed on my license. Yes, it was that

CHAPTER TWENTY

serious. I was not planning on going back to Mississippi anytime soon. So, for the next three days, we fell into a routine. Desmond would go to work while I stayed at home, waiting for him to get off so we could explore the city. I was living in the moment, trying to forget what I had left behind.

My phone hardly rang, and I did not answer when it did. It was not until the evening of the third day that my peace of mind ended. It just seemed like everyone started calling and texting my phone simultaneously. I did not want to talk to anyone. Apparently, my supervisor called my sister because I had not called in or anything. This behavior was very unusual for me because I loved my job. The funny thing is that I totally forgot all about even having a job. My mind was completely gone. Either way, I was not planning on going back. After a few hours of me ignoring everyone, Desmond's phone began to ring. It was the police.

After speaking to the detective, Desmond hung up and asked me, "What did you do?"

I explained to him that I did not tell anyone where I was or who I was with. Desmond did not have a clue about how I had utterly lost my mind and that everyone was worried about me. No one had seen or heard from me in three days, and my family had reported me missing. When the police finally got in contact with Desmond by way of my friends doing their own investigation, they told him to get me to a police station or that they would be busting down his door real soon. I was determined not to return to Mississippi, so I packed my things and headed to my car. My trip was over.

Desmond was not happy I had not been completely honest with him about why I suddenly wanted to come see him. However, at the same time, he was very concerned about me. Before he could talk me out of not leaving, I was gone and had no clue where I was going because I was in unfamiliar territory.

So, I drove until I saw an empty parking lot and just parked my car. I contemplated life yet again:

- What am I doing?
- Why won't everyone just leave me alone?
- Why do I have to go through this?
- Why can't I wake up from this nightmare?
- Why did you have to leave me, Craig?
- Why don't you just go ahead and kill yourself and be done?

Once again, I was stuck with just my thoughts, and it was not looking good at all. Desmond kept calling, and I finally decided to answer. He said he was in his car looking for me. So, the least I could do was suppress his worry by telling him where I was.

A few minutes later, Desmond showed up with his friend following behind him. We talked for just a few minutes, but when he started to tell me I needed to go to the hospital or police station, I completely lost it. I grabbed a bottle of sleeping pills I already had out and started walking to the other side of the car. He told me

CHAPTER TWENTY

he would not take me in, but I did not believe him. When he tried to grab me, I instantly shoved a handful of pills in my mouth and swallowed.

Immediately, his friend got out of his car while Desmond grabbed me and told me to spit the pills out, but they were already down my throat. I was just waiting for my body to react. His friend called the police. While we all waited for them to show, I became high and disoriented. Finally, I thought to myself. Finally, it would be over!

When the police and ambulance pulled up, I was completely out of it. All I remember was me telling them I did not need an ambulance and then falling out. I arrived at the hospital and heard the doctors and nurses telling each other I was the missing person. They told me there was a BOLO out for me, and I acted like I was in disbelief. I just wanted to get out of there. I did not want anything to do with what was happening. My mind could barely focus on them speaking to me. I was getting sleepier and sleepier by the minute until I just passed out while they were talking to me.

I woke up in a hospital room with an IV in my arm and a nurse in my room sitting down. I was somewhat out of it but was aware of where I was. I asked the nurse why she was just sitting there, and she told me I was on suicide watch. JUST GREAT! Now, I couldn't escape.

Not too long after, Desmond walked in, looking worn out. Poor guy. All he was trying to do was be a good friend, and it seems like I got him losing his mind as well. He said he did not get any sleep last night because he was up all night worried about me. He also said he was upset that his friend got arrested once I left in the ambulance last night. Once they ran his friend's name and saw he had active warrants, he went off to jail. What a night! He bent down to give me a kiss while sneaking me my phone. Since I was on suicide watch, I was not allowed a phone. Yet, here he was again, helping me despite what I had put him through.

Later on in the evening, two doctors came in and told me I would be moving to the psych ward and would be placed on a 72-hour psych evaluation hold. I told them I did not need that. They said I could either go voluntarily or involuntarily. I already knew what that meant when I saw the police officer in the back, rocking from side to side. I took the voluntary method for $200 please. It did not matter anyway. I had my phone and had plans to send a text real soon.

Chapter Twenty-One

And I said, Oh that I had wings like a dove! For then would I fly away, and be at rest.

PSALM 55:6 (KJV)

As I was rolled into the psych ward unit, I was met with a psychiatrist as well as other patients trying to speak to me. I already knew I would not be here long. She explained that I was on a 72-hour hold and could not make any phone calls until I signed myself in, saying I could not try to leave until the 72 hours were up. I was definitely not signing anything. Besides, I already knew how things were going to go. I mean, I was on the opposite side of the tracks here. It's wild how things have come full circle.

I was given a room number and told to come back out once I freshened up. I went to my room and immediately texted my dad when I went to the bathroom. Thankfully, I did not have a roommate, so I had privacy. My dad was very happy and thankful to hear from me after all that time. I could only imagine what was going through my parents' heads after receiving a call from the police that I was in the hospital all the way in Ohio. He texted that he and my sister had already booked a flight for later that night and would be at the hospital first thing in the morning.

The last thing he texted was, "DO NOT SIGN ANY PAPERWORK!"

I took a shower, laid down, and went to sleep. I made sure my phone was close to my body as I slept so no one would see it when they came in during the night to make their rounds.

Morning came fast, and I could tell the sleeping pills had completely worn off. I felt normal again and was ready to get up out of here. The psychiatrist met me as I was walking to a chair and informed me of the group activities they had planned for the day. I told her I was not interested and asked what time was visitation hours. She told me I could not have any visitors until I signed the 72-hour hold paperwork. I was very upset because I knew my family was coming to see me. I snuck off to the bathroom to text my dad, and he told me they told him the same thing when he called the hospital. We finally decided that the only option was for me to sign the paperwork to get them through the door, and then we would go from there.

After finally getting past all the red tape, I was allowed to see my dad and sister an hour later. Of course, my dad looked like he was about to cry, and yet again, I did not realize how my actions would affect those I loved. The psychiatrist came and introduced herself to my family, and come to find out, she was an AKA, just

CHAPTER TWENTY-ONE

like my sister. That information was a game changer. After finding this information out and telling her I was a psychology major, she felt compassion for me and decided to allow me to check myself out as long as I put myself under my dad's care. I also had to agree to have an evaluation done within 24 hours at the psych unit in my area. I agreed to these terms immediately.

Before I knew it, I was walking to the car with my family. The ride home was long, but we were all happy that I was safe and sound. I had to send out many texts to let everyone know I was okay. I honestly did not realize that many people cared about me. It felt good in a way, but the pain in my heart was undeniable. I was already working up my next play. I just did not know when or what it would be yet. All I knew was that the time was coming.

We were finally back home, and once again, I was in a bad state of mind. Just knowing I was back in Mississippi upset me all over again.

All I could think: I do not want to be here!

So, about a week later, it was on...

Chapter Twenty-Two

And they shall be gathered together, as prisoners are gathered in the pit, and shall be shut up in the prison, and after many days shall they be visited.

ISAIAH 24:22 (KJV)

I woke up and knew I was going to try suicide by cop again. I took half a bottle of Klonopin and got dressed in the same outfit as before. I got in the car, and just as I started to drive off, I received a call from the detective. I was hesitant to answer, but I did anyway. He said he was looking for my sister. I did not ask why, and honestly, I did not care. I told him he had the wrong number, then hung up.

I should have taken that as a sign to abort mission, but I was determined to see it through. So, I proceeded without caution. I started driving with no particular destination in mind. I just drove until the pills completely kicked in. I ended up in Ocean Springs and came upon another bank. Once again, I felt nothing. The pills were doing a fantastic job.

I got out of the car and walked right into the bank. Calm, cool, and collected. I asked for the money just like before. However, this time, a lady behind me yelled

CHAPTER TWENTY-TWO

and told me I needed to get out. She called me the devil several times and started rebuking me. I wanted to laugh because little did she know she was exactly right. I did have an evil spirit inside of me and wanted him to have his way. Brittnei been gone! I finally got the money and ran past the lady and her daughter out the door. She looked me dead in my eyes, and just for a split second, I felt convicted... But I kept running.

As I was running to my car, all of a sudden, the bag exploded. I was thrown into the air and hit the ground extremely hard. Smoke filled my lungs, and I could barely see. What happened? I was fighting for my life, but I still managed to grab the bag and make it to the car. I do not know how I was able to see while I drove off, but I did. I got off the main highway and took a back road so I could park and check my body for injuries. Once I parked, I realized my fingers were bleeding because I broke my nail down to the skin when I fell. I also realized I scraped my knee during the fall as well.

However, the most obvious problem I had was the fact that I had red dye all over me. That was the cause of the explosion. The teller put a dye pack inside my bag. Lucky for me, I had a change of clothes in the car. So I changed right there in the parking lot. Soon, I was back on the road.

I was still high on the pills, which is why I do not know how I ended up at my friend Keisha's house or even the route I took to get there. All I know is she let me in. I did not immediately tell her what happened, but she instantly knew something was wrong. Once I pulled the money out, she understood what was going on. Her eyes became huge, but she didn't say anything. Not too long after arriving, my phone began to ring. Everyone was calling me, and I did not feel like answering. Keisha decided to check and see if anything was on the news, and there I was, front and center.

My face was plastered everywhere with the caption: BREAKING NEWS!

I had made the mistake of not pulling the turtleneck up over my face. I had messed up big time. I just shrugged my shoulders and accepted the fact that I would let the police shoot me like I wanted in the first place. Problem solved. Keisha asked me how I was so calm, and I told her I was high on pills. She told me to give her the money so she could hide it for me. I felt it was a good idea at the time, so I agreed.

Not too long after, I left and headed back home. I did not get far out of the apartment complex because, unbeknownst to me, the police had traced my phone and were waiting for me to come out of the apartment. I only got down the street when the flashing lights came on. My car was surrounded by cops within seconds. I looked to the right side of my car and saw that a policeman was already approaching my car. All I could do was smile because I knew this was it. It was my time to shine.

They instructed me to turn the car off and to get out with my hands up. I looked down at my phone and planned on using it as a gun to run towards the police,

CHAPTER TWENTY-TWO

but at that very moment, the most unbelievable thing happened. A blurry vision of my mom appeared right before me, and I knew I could not go through with it. I knew my mom would rather see me in jail than see me in a casket. There was no way I could carry out my plan now. So, I did exactly what they asked me to do and got out with my hands up.

They did not even make me get on the ground, nor were they rough. They handcuffed me and made me stand by a police car as they searched my car. I do not know why, but I suddenly became very aggravated and impatient. I was ready for them to hurry up and do whatever it was they were going to do with me. Finally, it was time to go to jail. Instead of putting me in the back seat, the officers put me in the front seat and buckled me up in the police car. When we got to the police station, I was fingerprinted and put in the interrogation room. I watched enough of the ID channel to know what was coming next.

I do not know how long they made me wait, but I instantly denied everything when they finally came in and asked questions. I was actually mad at the detectives for trying to insult my intelligence. They really thought I was going to fold under pressure. Not to mention, I would not do their job for them. So, all the yelling they did was in vain. They kept making threats that went in one ear and out the other. I believe I was getting under their skin rather than them getting under mine. I made them work hard that night. After what felt like an eternity of back and forth, I asked if I could finally leave, and that sent them over the edge.

They yelled, "No!" more than once to my face. They were firm in letting me know that I was not going anywhere. So, I told them to take me to the back then. They asked me again if I was sure I did not want to make a statement, and then it was my turn to yell, "No!" at them. I did not want to talk, so I sat in silence. That was my answer.

When I got to the back and put in the cell with three other women, I just looked at them. No one said anything to me, and I did not say anything to them. I just climbed on the top rack and went straight to sleep. That was some of the best sleep I had gotten in a long time. It's crazy how I finally found some peace in a jail cell of all places.

Chapter Twenty-Three

He who covers his sins will not prosper, But whoever confesses and forsakes them will have mercy.

PROVERBS 28:13 (NKJV)

I woke up to the guards telling me I had a visitor. Great! I walked into the same interrogation room, and there was my dad and aunt. I was not expecting this. I was handcuffed behind my back, so I was not allowed to hug them. My dad looked heartbroken and tired. We talked for a few seconds, and then in walked the same detectives from the night before.

By the time the cops were done with the good cop/bad cop role, they realized some serious mental problems were going on with me. They offered me food and drinks, but I did not accept anything. I was still mad from the night before. My mood instantly changed, and I was back to being cold. They tried talking to me again and asked me nicely if I had anything to say, but I would not budge. Then, my dad finally asked me if I really did it, and my heart softened a bit. I folded like a glove. I told them everything. They asked about the first robbery, and

I admitted to that one as well. I was actually relieved everything was out on the table. It was becoming too much to keep such a heavy secret. They allowed me to talk to my dad and aunt a little longer. After that, they escorted me back to my cell.

When I made it back, all of the ladies were up, and once again, they were just looking at me. Finally, one of them asked if I was really the lady who robbed the banks. I was shocked that they heard about it without having a television. I'm unsure how the news trickled in, but I had no reason to lie.

I told them, "Yes, it was me."

No big deal, right? Wrong! They were so excited and made me feel like I was a celebrity. They asked me questions, and I answered every one of them. I also told them what led up to everything. They were all stone-cold silent. Wow! I did not realize how telling them the entire story would affect a person as well. With the ice broken, we all seemed to get along just fine.

Adjusting to the ladies was cool, but adjusting to being in jail proved to be a challenging task for me. There is absolutely no privacy. You are told what to do, when to do it, and how to do it. You are told when to eat, sleep, shower, make phone calls, have visits, and sometimes when to use the bathroom. Not to mention, you can't even use the bathroom in private when you use it.

I could not believe this was my life at the moment, but I could do nothing about it. The only good thing about

CHAPTER TWENTY-THREE

the situation was that the guards were actually cool and not aggressive, as shown on television. That eased some of the discomfort. Though, things were about to shift once more. GOD can use even our low points to make something miraculous.

About three days into my stay, I received a Bible and reading materials from my family. The other ladies did not have anything so I decided to do Bible study with them. Even through all of this, GOD's Word remained in me. Every night, this became our routine. I would sit on the bottom rack while the other ladies made a circle around me on the floor. I would do a Bible study lesson with them and then read a chapter from one of my reading books. They all loved this because it allowed us to escape these walls for a while, even if it was just in our heads. They were also very eager to learn more about GOD's Word. During this time, I also began teaching them the Lord's Prayer.

Before I knew it, two weeks passed, and it was time to go to court. The ladies asked me to pray for them the night before we were all scheduled to go to court. I felt honored because of the respect they had for me, even though we were all in the same situation. Afterward, one of the ladies came up to me and said she had finally memorized the Lord's Prayer and wanted to recite it to me. I felt like a proud mom when she finished. She was so excited as well and said she could not wait to get home and teach her children. The next day, I was in court. I walked in and saw my dad and aunt yet again. We were there for a bond reduction, and thank GOD we got it. It went from $250,000 to $50,000. I was allowed to visit with them again, and my dad still looked like he was struggling with the entire situation. I asked him if it was on the news, and he said it was broadcast everywhere. Everyone knew what I had done.

I was not expecting to hear that, but unfortunately, many unexpected things have been happening to me lately. My dad also told me my sister was expecting again. For the first time in a while, I smiled. At least that was some good news during all of this. A lot was going through my mind as I returned to my cell after my visit. However, I did not have time to sit and dwell on everything.

Within an hour, I was saying goodbye to the ladies, and it was a surprisingly sad moment. I was then handcuffed again and escorted to a police car. I had to get transported to another facility due to the robberies being in two different counties. I had to go through the whole booking process again. When I arrived and finally made it to the back of this new facility, a woman ran up to the door and yelled, "You're my shero! I'm your number one fan!"

I just shook my head. No one knew me. No one knew my story. No one knew my background. This was not me. I still could not wrap my head around how women thought this was cool.

Although I spent another two weeks there, just like at the other facility, it seemed like these two weeks went

CHAPTER TWENTY-THREE

by incredibly slowly. Not to mention, there were way more females. I got into a routine of doing my own Bible Study, but here they had someone from the outside to come and do Bible Study as well. I wasn't sure what to make of my situation, but I received some news while at this new facility.

A few days after I arrived, a woman approached me about my friend Keisha. She asked me if I had heard that Keisha had been arrested. I was shocked to hear this information. She continued by saying that Keisha had been charged with accessory after the fact and that she had just bonded out a few hours before I came. I felt so bad. I had no idea they would even think about going after her. It had not been my intention to make things difficult for Keisha, and at that time, I could only hope she was doing okay.

At the second facility, I got along with the ladies, but I pretty much stayed to myself most of the time. Besides, I was not here to make friends. I was ready to go home. After another two weeks, I was once again headed to court for another bond reduction. This time, my bond went from $150,000 to $60,000. This reduction was yet another blessing. I needed to go home since I had developed a nasty eye infection. I'm sure it was because jail is very unsanitary. It is basically a step up from living in your own filth. Yeah, I was ready to go.

I bonded out on my 29th birthday and took that as my birthday gift. It was the best gift I could have ever received at that time. As I walked out the jail doors, I was happy to finally be able to smell fresh air. I felt like I had been locked up for months instead of weeks. I hugged my dad like I had never hugged him before. As we made it to the car, I felt like this gave my dad some relief, knowing his baby girl was coming home.

As we got in the car and began to drive home, the song "Strong Man" by Shirley Caesar was playing. I started to listen to the words. As soon as she said, "And he's holding on to someone's daughter too," I immediately broke down, and tears filled my eyes. At this very moment, I realized I was the daughter the devil was holding onto, and I knew it. My dad turned the volume up as loud as it could go so I could listen to the song loud and clear. We drove home with me crying the entire way.

Chapter Twenty-Four

To every thing there is a season, and a time to every purpose under the heaven: a time to get, and a time to lose; a time to keep, and a time to cast away;

ECCLESIASTES 3:1,6 (KJV)

When we finally made it home, my mom looked like she was going through it. I felt so bad for her, but she said she was happy that I was finally home and that she could calm her nerves. My sister was there too with a birthday cake. My mom then told me something came in the mail for me. It was a birthday card from Sharon, out of all people.

It read, "Happy Birthday. I hope you are able to enjoy your day. Let me know if you need anything."

Instantly, I got upset. I tore up the card and threw it in the trash. I wanted to scream, "I NEEDED YOU! What do you mean?!" When I needed her, she threatened to call the police. No, I did not need anything from her. I could not believe she would send me that card after everything. Sure, I had been civil at the hospital when I saw her, but it did not mean I had forgotten what she had done. I chose not to dwell on it, knowing I needed to focus on what was ahead of me.

That night, my mom was in my room with me, watching me pack a bag for the next day. I had been court-ordered to go inpatient as part of my bond agreement. So, the very next day, I went inpatient at the mental health facility. Here I was with a mental health degree, being admitted into the mental health facility yet again. What are the odds?

The first day, they had to do a psych evaluation on me. Of course, I was familiar with the questions because they were the same ones my clients had to answer. I was then told of the daily activities I had to participate in, and so forth. The very same day, we had a group discussion, and everyone had to introduce themselves to me, and I had to do the same. It was simple, and I knew I needed to go along with it without too much fuss.

Once we went on lunch break, a guy approached me and asked if I was the lady in the picture as he was holding up the newspaper. I just looked at the paper, knowing full well that it was me. I finally said yes, and he said he was amazed at how calm I was. He told me what was said in the paper about me, and I told him everything that happened leading up to me being there with him. He explained that he understood all too well about PTSD since he, too, was suffering through it being in the military. After that conversation, we instantly became friends. He said that I was the first person he was able to have a decent conversation with since he had been there. After a day or two, I understood what he meant.

CHAPTER TWENTY-FOUR

Some people walked around talking to themselves. Some were way older than me and were walking around with dolls. Some were making threats towards others. Then, there were some who did not talk at all.

The craziest thing I experienced while there was a guy who would constantly make threats towards people because he had Tourette's syndrome. One day, he told me he wanted to skin me like a fish. Out of all the things he had said to me, this was the worst, and it made my skin crawl. So, I turned around and repeated it back to him. I told him I wanted to skin him like a fish.

He got so mad and asked, "Why would you say that?"

I asked him the same question.

He said, "Well, I have Tourette's, and I can't help it."

So I said, "Who knows, I might have Tourette's, too."

I laughed at myself because I knew I was completely losing my mind if I was sitting there arguing with another mental patient. I went and told my only friend, and we laughed together. I felt like we were the only sane people there. We had gotten really close in just a few days. I thought I had an ally for the duration of my stay.

Until one day, I saw him sitting at the end of the hall, balled up, crying. As I walked towards him, I called his name. He looked up and told me he did not want to talk. I asked him if he was okay, and he said no. I told him I would give him some space for the time being but would be back in a few minutes to check on him. That time never came. Not too long after that, two military men in full uniform, marching in sync with one another, came in and took my friend away. No words were spoken, and there were no goodbyes. He cried the entire way out. I never knew what happened to him.

Then, a week later, I was discharged because of my insurance. My insurance had expired since I was immediately terminated from my job after I got arrested. I was not mad when my job discharged me because I felt like the longer I stayed, the worse my mental health would become. So, instead, I would start outpatient therapy the following week.

Once I made it home, my parents made it their business to keep an eye on me at all times. I could not blame them. Honestly, I could not trust myself. I was so far gone mentally that I did not know what I was capable of. After a few months, I was finally allowed some freedom and took advantage of it.

I returned to all my social media platforms and found out that another of my so-called "friends," Diona, had deleted me from all her social media accounts. I just laughed at the fact that sometimes, when you need your loved ones the most, they show their true colors. When you hit rock bottom, you find out who your true friends are. As hard as it is to say, I needed to see that. Luckily, I still have three friends who have remained loyal throughout this difficult time in my life. They knew my situation and did not judge or look at me differently. I needed to see that as well.

I ended up making an online dating profile and

CHAPTER TWENTY-FOUR

started online dating. I guess you can call it speed dating because I was going on a date almost every night. I was not trying to find love at the time. I was trying to keep my mind occupied. I was also meeting random guys, hoping one would kidnap me and kill me. I know it sounds ridiculous, but this was how I felt then. I just wanted the pain to end. I wanted my life to end. I was always out drinking and partying, just not even worried about the seriousness of the charges over my head.

During this time, I was back and forth to court, not knowing what the outcome would be. All I knew was that I had this dark cloud hovering over my head, and yet, here I was, living it up like no tomorrow. I would go out, get drunk, and drive home, hoping I would drive into a tree or something. I was completely out of control. I knew it was only a matter of time before I wrecked and added to my many problems.

One day, I decided to take a chance and go over to Keisha's house since we had not spoken since we were arrested. To my surprise, she was standing outside. I asked her about the money, and she said she and Lauryn had burned it. I was shocked and confused, but at the time, I had no choice but to believe her. So, I left it at that. I apologized to her for putting her through all of that, and she said she was good. We started back hanging out, and everything was cool for a while.

Something else I was concerned about was that I started to gain weight. I did not realize how big I had gotten until I stood next to my mom and sister while we took a picture. I could not believe my eyes when I looked at the picture. I was huge and way bigger than the two of them. I guess all the heavy drinking and going out to eat every night had finally caught up with me. I had gotten up to 230 pounds. So, when I looked at myself in the mirror, I was disgusted. It only added to my depression. When I thought things could not get any worse, they did.

I was always doped up on the many medications they had me on for my anxiety and depression. Not to mention, I was already on different other medications for my lupus. Sometimes, I could barely function. There were also times when I would just zone out. My mind would go elsewhere, and sometimes, my parents would have to snap me out of it. Unfortunately, there came a time when they could not be there to snap me out of it.

One day, while I was driving, I zoned out. I ended up running a red light and ran into the side of someone. The accident was so bad that I was taken to the hospital. The car, my mom's car, was completely totaled. Just great. Not only could I have possibly injured someone, but I totaled my mom's car as well. I really just wanted everything to be over. Thankfully, I was not injured, nor was the driver I hit.

At this point, my parents did not know what to do with me. They saw my life spiraling out of control and had no clue how to help me. I did not even know how to help myself, so I had nothing to offer them as a resolve. I wanted out of my misery, and they wanted to help me

CHAPTER TWENTY-FOUR

find my way back from the edge. The only thing they knew to do was pray. AND PRAY THEY DID!

Shortly after the wreck, I began to get antsy. I needed to get out of the house because the walls were beginning to close in on me. I told Keisha, and she started coming to get me and even allowed me to use her car sometimes. But, eventually, she stopped answering and, out of nowhere, cut off all communication. I took it quite well this time because I had gotten used to people turning their backs on me by that point. So, she was no exception. But we all know that what goes on in the dark will eventually come to light. Just wait for it.

Chapter Twenty-Five

For which I suffer hardship even to imprisonment as a criminal, but the word of GOD is not inprisoned.

2 TIMOTHY 2:9

AUGUST 17, 2018. It was my birthday, and I felt nervous for the first time since all of this had begun. In a way, I somehow knew what the outcome would be. I accepted the fact that this could very well be my last birthday on the outside for a while. Although I still hoped that a miracle could happen, I still had to be honest with myself. I mean, I did rob two banks. So, I tried to enjoy myself as best as I could, but the truth is, I was ready for all of this to be over with. All I could do was wait and see what was in store.

OCTOBER 4, 2018

Finally, the day had come. After two years of being out on bond, I was in court for sentencing. I was finally pleading guilty to the charge of armed robbery. This entire time, the prosecuting attorney had been asking the judge to give me 15 years to life for my crime. I was afraid that he could possibly get what he wanted. But

CHAPTER TWENTY-FIVE

to my surprise, this particular prosecutor was not there when we came to court. A few weeks before my court date, he was given another assignment and taken off my case. This was when I knew GOD had not taken His hand off of me.

On top of that, none of the witnesses that agreed to testify against me showed up. Things were going in my favor in court, surprisingly. My hope continued to climb when the judge spoke to my lawyer and me. He explained that he agreed that I had a mental breakdown. I began to cry because I realized he had compassion towards me. Something I heard was the complete opposite about him. After he gave his empathic speech, he finally sent down his sentence:

3 YEARS AT THE MISSISSIPPI DEPARTMENT OF CORRECTIONS. (MANDATORY)

Immediately, I hit the floor, and everything went black. While it may not have been exactly what I wanted, GOD still shielded me from what it could have been. The sentencing brought an end to this tumultuous chapter of my life, giving me the chance to start anew.

My Testimony

On March 24, 2024, I was asked to speak at church. Of course, I was nervous at first, but I also felt like it was time to give my testimony, which is what I did. Afterward, I went into my lesson entitled: *"Taking Medicine For Someone Else"* (2 Corinthians 1:3-7).

GOD OF ALL COMFORT

GOD has not promised us a bed of roses. Even if that were true, we must remember that roses come with thorns. Life is a battlefield, and war has its victims, which, at times, could even be one of us. People go through things every day, including Christians. Stress and suffering are no respecter of person. So, one of the greatest needs today is real solid COMFORT!

Trials and tribulations fall on everyone. This fact means that trouble, heartache, pain, stress, grief, etc., fall on the just as well as the unjust. It falls on the godly as well as the ungodly. But what helps ease those unpleasant feelings and that suffering is comfort. The word "comfort" will be mentioned quite a few times today.

Comfort: The pleasant and satisfying feeling of being physically or mentally free from pain and suffering, or something that provides this feeling.

Comfort is something we all seek. It is something we all long for. But where does this source of comfort come from? There is only one answer. Paul explains in 2 Corinthians 1:3 that:

1. GOD is the Father of our Lord Jesus Christ.
2. GOD is the Father of mercies.
3. GOD is the GOD of all comfort.

Paul is someone who can speak on comfort as he suffered many trials and tribulations. Here's a little background on Paul:

- He was born in Tarsus.
- He was a tent maker.
- He was a trained Pharisee.
- Previously known as Saul, he was on the road to Damascus when he had an encounter with Jesus.

We all can agree that once you have an encounter with Jesus, your life will never be the same. That's what happened with Paul. Before his conversion to Christianity, Paul had been a Pharisee who intensely persecuted followers of Jesus. GOD allowed him to change when he went from Saul to Paul. After Paul's conversion:

- He became a faithful man of GOD.
- He established many churches.
- He preached the gospel.
- He wrote many letters, which the church still uses.

These scriptures were the beginning of a letter that Paul had written to the Corinthian church. Now, Paul wrote these letters to see how the church was doing and to comfort them.

The idea behind the word "comfort" is to give strength, to give help, and to make one strong. So, basically, Paul wanted to encourage the people of Corinth. 2 Corinthians 1:4 (NKJV) says, "*Who comforts us in all our tribulation.*"

As I previously stated, "*Roses come with thorns,*" meaning trouble will come, and problems will arise. But thank GOD for being our comforter during our trials and tribulations. Verse 4 continues, "*So that we may be able to comfort them which are in any trouble, by the comfort wherewith we ourselves are comforted of GOD.*" So that same comfort GOD gives us through those stormy days and sleepless nights, we are to pass on to someone who is worried, burdened, and going through what you have already been through. Sometimes, we are simply taking medicine for someone else.

Think about it: "How can you help somebody who's

going through it if you have never been through it?" The purpose of receiving GOD's comfort is not just for yourself. The purpose is not only for us but to be passed on to someone else in need. The Bible teaches us in Galatians that we are to bear one another's burden. We are to intercede on behalf of others. We are taking medicine for someone else.

Now, there is some suffering we endure simply because we are hardheaded and do what we want to do. But the sufferings in 2 Corinthians 1:5 speaks on the suffering of Christ: "For as the sufferings of Christ abound in us, so our consolation also abounds through Christ." (NKJV) Why is this important to note?

We all know that Paul had a life filled with much suffering. He described some of these sufferings in 2 Corinthians 11: 23-28:
- prison
- beatings
- stoning
- shipwrecked
- perils of waters
- robbers

Sometimes, I, too, felt like Paul. I've been through many hardships in my 36 years of life. Most of the time, when Paul was writing these letters, he was going through something. He was suffering, but yet and still, he was strong enough to provide comfort to the churches. Again, 2 Corinthians 1:5 (NKJV): *"So our consolation also abounds through Christ."*

Do you know how hard it is to encourage someone when you are fighting your own battles and dealing with your own problems? I was in prison, trying to help those women and give them comfort, all the while I was going through it myself. But GOD, my comforter, kept me strong. He kept me motivated. He kept me encouraged, giving me the strength to continue on the mission I was on. NOBODY BUT GOD!

2 Corinthians 1:6 (NKJV) begins, "*Now if we are afflicted, it is for your consolation and salvation,*" In this verse, Paul was saying that if he and the other ministers had to suffer, it would be for the benefit and salvation of God's people (the Corinthian church). As suffering brought Paul closer to GOD and made him rely on GOD more and more, he became a more effective minister and leader. The stronger your relationship with GOD is, the stronger your faith will be, and that will strengthen your testimony. Paul was willing to take that medicine for someone else.

2 Corinthians 1:6 (NKJV) continues, "*which is effective for enduring the same sufferings which we also suffer.*" Paul was saying here that everyone's problems are not the same. What may be an issue for me may not be an issue for you. But regardless of the circumstances, for one reason or another, we will face some difficult times. We should never get into a competition to compare suffering. When I got to prison, I looked at my timesheet and saw that I had three years. I was so angry and started to complain. But as time went on, I realized

that my three years were nothing compared to most of the women in there. Some had 15 years, 20 years, and some even had a life sentence. So, like the song says, "I won't complain." I won't complain because that could have been me.

2 Corinthians 1:6 (NKJV) finishes with: "*Or if we are comforted, it is for your consolation and salvation.*" Throughout the verses, Paul mainly talked about how GOD used him through his suffering. But in this verse, Paul was saying how GOD can also use us when things are going well. That's why you may hear people say, GOD blesses you to be a blessing to others. Whatever GOD gives you, you are to share it with others. Why? Because your going-through might be my been-through. In sharing my testimony, it might help you get through.

2 Corinthians 1:7 (NKJV) says, "*And our hope for you is steadfast, because we know that as you are partakers of the sufferings, so also you will partake of the consolation.*" Paul told the Corinthian church that since they were sharing in the suffering and bearing one another's burdens, they would also share in the comfort. Romans 12:15 (KJV) says, "Rejoice with them that do rejoice, and weep with them that weep." And during those times of weeping, we are to console one another. Comfort one another. That comfort is in the CROSS, which always guarantees everything we need! That very same comfort comes from GOD Himself, who sent His only Son to "Take medicine for someone else." Medicine that was meant for you and me.

But we were not fit to take the medicine. Jesus, who knew no sin, had to take on the sins of the entire world. Isaiah 53:4-5 (KJV) tells us, *"Surely he hath borne our griefs, and carried our sorrows: yet we did esteem him stricken, smitten of God, and afflicted. But he was wounded for our transgressions, he was bruised for our iniquities: the chastisement of our peace was upon him."* Meaning Jesus was beaten just for me. Then, they placed a crown of thorns on His head to mock Him. They even pressed it down into His head to hurt Him. No matter how nasty that medicine tasted, He knew He had to take it. The same people that were once shouting, "Hosanna, Hosanna," were now shouting, "Crucify, crucify."

Through it all, He never said a mumbling word. He was marched up to a hill called Calvary, where He was hung on a Cross. All the way to the end, Jesus knew He had to take this medicine for someone else. Then, after He gave up the ghost, they pierced Him in His side. Blood and water came streaming down. They then took Him off the Cross and laid Him in a borrowed tomb. He stayed there all night Friday and Saturday, but EARLY Sunday morning, He rose with all power in His Hand!

ALL BECAUSE HE HAD TO TAKE THAT MEDICINE FOR YOU AND FOR ME.

As I said before, GOD had me on a mission while I was in prison, and when I came home, that mission was complete. But that's the thing: that "mission" is complete. That doesn't mean GOD didn't have something else for me to do. I soon realized that. Not even two weeks ago, my close friend needed me. The same friend that was there for me when my boyfriend passed away. The same friend that was there the entire time I was in prison. The same friend, who waited until I came home just so I could be in her wedding, lost her husband the same way I lost my boyfriend. He had a massive heart attack and died right in front of her. I took that medicine for her eight years ago. GOD knew this day would come, and He knew I would be strong enough to help and comfort her with the same comfort He gave me.

So, you never know when you have to take medicine for someone else.

The Chosen One

As I sit in my cell all alone
And wonder when this pain will end.
Will I ever come to terms with my situation
Or will I ever see the light of day again?

I continued to ask myself more questions
then decided this is how it's supposed to be.
But one particular question still remained
I asked, "Lord, why'd you choose me?"

Lord, why was I the child
that seemed to never get it right?
Why was I the one chosen
to have every hardship in sight?

Why was I the sick one
Always having to take meds?
Having pain that would be so bad,
all I could do was lay in bed.

Lord, why was I the child
that couldn't finish out my dream?
All I wanted to do was play ball
and enjoy the happiness it brings.

THE CHOSEN ONE

But that also didn't go as planned.
I was told my dream must end.
I would think back and grin
about how bad luck had become my friend.

Why was I the child
who couldn't find the perfect mate?
And when I thought I'd finally found him,
You had to come and take.

Lord, why was I the one
with mental problems no one understood?
Not knowing how to ask for help
and taking more meds that did no good.

Why did I go all the way left
And had to deal with bitterness and strife?
Lord, why did you even intervene
when I tried to take my own life?

Finally, the Lord answered and said,
"My child, why can't you see?
This path has nothing to do with you
because it's all about Me!

I chose you to have sickness
to show others it doesn't mean death.
I knew you'd be able to handle it
no matter how bad you felt.

As for playing ball
I chose to make your time short.
I had many families that needed
your love, care, and support.

GOD IS KEEPING ME

You say you have bad luck,
I guess you've forgotten the many days
that even in the worst of times,
things could have still been the other way.

I took your "perfect mate"
because he wasn't yours to keep.
I had work for him to do as well.
So, his maker he had to meet.

Your time will come again someday
When you'll find love like no other.
I promise I'll send your "soulmate"
Just like I did your sister and brother.

I chose you to study mental health
because I knew this illness would arrive.
I even knew how unstable you'd become,
But I also knew you'd still survive.

Your life is not your own
and with the many times you've tried to escape.
Have you ever stopped and asked yourself,
"Is my life really mine to take?"

I chose you for this mission
And blessings you will gain.
While doing the Lord's Will,
you're bringing glory to MY Name!"

About the Author

Brittnei Michelle Farmer was born on August 17, 1987, in Gulfport, MS, to the proud parents of Ed and Jackie Farmer. She was the second of three children. Brittnei was a very bubbly child with a kind heart who could make friends with anyone. At an early age, Brittnei showed interest in sports, particularly softball, and basketball. By the age of 10, she was not only playing league softball, but she was also playing all-star softball ball as well. As she juggled softball, basketball, and school, she enjoyed spending time with her family the most. Although Brittnei was diagnosed with Lupus at the age of 12, she did not let that stop her from continuing with her love for sports. This strength and determination to persevere during hard times would prove to be her driving force later in life with the obstacles she would face.

Brittnei gave her life to Christ at the tender age of 13 at Shiloh Missionary Baptist Church in Saucier, MS, where she was an active member. By the time Brittnei reached high school, she was already on track to receive many softball scholarships. However, after a traumatic knee injury during her sophomore year, Brittnei's potential scholarships were removed from the table one by one. However, Brittnei returned after a year and still received a softball scholarship to Mississippi Gulf Coast Community College in Perkinston, Mississippi.

Brittnei received her Associate's in General Studies, but her softball career was over after another traumatic knee injury during the last game of her freshman year. Although this was devasting for Brittnei, she soon realized that her plans were not God's.

In 2009, while going through a troubling breakup with a boyfriend, Brittnei suffered a life-threatening illness after a staph infection developed into sepsis. After a year recovering, Brittnei became a powerful vessel for GOD. She became a Sunday school teacher, a youth advisory, a member of the prayer band, was on the usher board, and joined the women's choir. Brittnei was in church every time the church doors opened. Also, during this time, after taking a year off from school to try to recover, Brittnei obtained her bachelor's in psychology from William Carey University in 2011. She was soon offered a child and family case manager position at Mississippi Children's Homes Services.

Finally, Brittnei realized her calling. She genuinely loved others and desired to help those in need. In 2012, Brittnei fell in love with who she thought would be her forever partner, and they were together for 4 years until GOD decided to call him home in 2016. Of all the obstacles Brittnei has had to face, this was something she could not handle, and she made a life-altering decision

ABOUT THE AUTHOR

that ultimately landed her in prison for 3 years. You might find it hard to believe, but this is where Brittnei needed to be to find herself. Although she was in therapy for a few years to recover from her life-altering experience with death, here she is today, standing tall with her head held high. She had to lose friends and family members along the way, but most importantly, she did not lose her FAITH!

Today, Brittnei wishes to share her story with you and others to let everyone know that despite what it may look like, GOD IS STILL IN CONTROL!! Everything happens for a reason, and GOD will reveal everything in His time. We just have to trust Him.

Today, Brittnei Manages the Family Business, and she enjoys spending time with her family, especially her nieces (Kourtlynn, Kamdynn, and Briar). As well as her goddaughter, Evelyn. Brittnei is still an active member of Shiloh Missionary Baptist Church and takes great pride in giving her testimony every chance she gets. She finds a sense of gratitude when encouraging and motivating others. Brittnei also enjoys writing poems, singing, and playing with all 5 of her pets (dogs). She has plans to write part 2 of her memoir detailing her prison stay. She also plans to become a motivational speaker in the near future.

Connect with the Author

Brittnei looks forward to connecting with you! For updates on new book releases, speaking engagements, and more, check out the information below.

INSTAGRAM   bfarmer_19
FACEBOOK   Brittnei Farmer
TIKTOK   @bfarmer19
EMAIL   brittneifarmer007@gmail.com

www.ingramcontent.com/pod-product-compliance
Lightning Source LLC
Chambersburg PA
CBHW071121090426
42736CB00012B/1972